A TIME TO READ

A Time to Read
Good Books for Growing Readers

Mary Ruth K. Wilkinson
& Heidi Wilkinson Teel

REGENT COLLEGE PUBLISHING
VANCOUVER, BRITISH COLUMBIA

A Time to Read
Copyright © 2001 by Mary Ruth K. Wilkinson
and Heidi Wilkinson Teel

Published 2001 by Regent College Publishing,
an imprint of the Regent College Bookstore,
5800 University Boulevard, Vancouver, B.C. Canada V6T 2E4

The views expressed in works published by
Regent College Publishing
are those of the author and may not necessarily
represent the official position of Regent College.

The paper used in this publication meets the minimum
requirements of the American National Standard for Information
Sciences—Permanence of Paper for Printed Library Materials,
ANSI Z39.48-1984.

Canadian Cataloguing in Publication Data

Wilkinson, Mary Ruth K., 1942–
A time to read

ISBN 0-88865-448-0 (Canada)
ISBN 1-57383-146-8 (United States)

1. Children's literature—Bibliography. 2. Children—Books and reading.
3. Best books. 4. Christian literature for children—Bibliography.
I. Wilkinson Teel, Heidi, 1967– II. Title.
Z1037.W46 2001   011.62   C00-910500-X

Dedicated with love to
Daughters / Granddaughters
Esther-Ruth Galadriel Teel
and Elanor Anna Wilkinson Teel

"Children are the living messages
we send to a time we will not see."
—Neil Postman,
THE DISAPPEARANCE OF CHILDHOOD

Contents

Preface

What fun it is to put together a booklist: remembering favourites, reading new discoveries, perusing bookstores, bringing home bags of books from the library, and having a chance to talk about children's books with family, friends, neighbours, and anybody else who will listen!

However, in putting together this booklist, we have found ourselves limited in two major ways: first, in keeping up with the children's books that are continually being published; second, in being aware of how soon so many great books become out-of-print and unavailable (often to make room for newer, not-so-good books). We have decided to include some "unavailable books" (in the hopes that you can find them) and some readily available "out-of-print" books as well. For some help, see "Sources of Good Books" in **Helps Along the Way to Good Books for Children**.

There is a third limit which we have placed upon ourselves: scope. We have limited ourselves to books we know and love, books we think qualify as literature, books that tell good stories. Even so, that has left us (and you!) with over 750 books to think about.

This book starts with an essay (**Restorying**) on *why* we should be reading to our children and encouraging them to read as well. It continues with a practical guide (**Introducing your Children to Books**) for *how* to start reading to young children, followed by the annotated list of **Picture Books**. Next, we move on to chapters on **Music** and **Poetry**, including discussions of their importance and suggested readings.

In the center or core of the book is the **Bible Stories** section, with suggestions for all ages.

With this perspective on Biblical knowledge behind us we move to the longer books—books for children who are able to listen to "chapter" books and/or read for themselves: **Fairy Tales and Mythology, Fantasy and Science Fiction, Animal Stories, Historical Fiction, Good Stories, Prolific Authors for Avid Readers,** and **Alternatives to "Young Adult" Fiction.**

Next comes a chapter (**Helps Along the Way to Good Books for Children**) which includes a discussion of censorship, several lists of books to buy as gifts (as well as where to find them), ideas for family reading, and suggested readings for the continued study of children's literature.

The book ends with two sections: **References**, filled with information (sources and commentary) regarding the quotes used in this book, and a three-part **Index** listing books by author, by illustrator and by title.

For us, the cover art (*The Grandmother Tree* by Rose Mewhort) symbolizes many of the elements necessary for growth: deep roots, weathered storms, and the wisdom of grandmothers! We hope you take time to read this book and fill it with your own notes, and may the wisdom of many "grandmothers" deepen your roots and the roots of your children.

Thank you to the students through the years in the Regent College *Books, Children and God* class, and to Sheila Egoff, Patricia Hill, Barbara Abrahams, Heather Page (and her family!), Susan Norman, and Erik Wilkinson for all their book recommendations and wisdom. We are especially grateful to our husbands, Loren Wilkinson and Paul Teel, for helpful and decisive feedback when we couldn't make up our minds, for encouraging support when we were ready to flag, and for hours of editing and proofreading, of typing and entering corrections. They have husbanded us well!

—*Mary Ruth Wilkinson*
& Heidi Wilkinson Teel

I can only answer the question 'What am I to do?' if I can answer the prior question 'Of what story or stories do I find myself a part?' We enter human society, that is, with one or more imputed characters—roles into which we have been drafted—and we have to learn what they are in order to be able to understand how others respond to us and how our responses to them are apt to be construed. It is through hearing stories about wicked stepmothers, lost children, good but misguided kings, wolves that suckle twin boys, youngest sons who receive no inheritance but must make their own way in the world . . . that children learn or mis-learn both what a child and what a parent is, what the cast of characters may be in the drama in which they have been born and what the ways of the world are. Deprive children of stories and you leave them unscripted, anxious stutterers in their actions as in their words.

—Alasdair MacIntyre

All themes and characters and stories that you encounter in literature belong to one big interlocking family . . . in literature you don't just read one poem after another, but enter into a complete world of which every work of literature forms a part.

—Northrop Frye

1

Re*story*ing

Never before have we had at our fingertips such a wealth of information. But information isn't wisdom. It isn't even knowledge. To make sense of all those facts we need stories. As Alasdair MacIntyre puts it in AFTER VIRTUE:

> It is through hearing stories that children [and adults] learn or mis-learn both what a child and what a parent is, what the cast of characters may be in the drama in which they have been born and what the ways of the world are . . . . Deprive children of stories and you leave them unscripted, anxious stutterers.

And we do have lots of stories today. Think of a Saturday morning's cartoons on TV, or a week's worth of TV movies and serial "episodes." Think of dozens of "Sweet Valley High" and "Goosebumps" books. But what's missing in this flood of stories is precisely what our contemporary culture is intent on denying: a "Story of stories" to guide us and our children through a maze in which all stories are seen to be equally true (or false).

Christians believe that there is a Story of stories. We encounter it wordlessly and mysteriously in creation, and we encounter it much more directly in the Bible, which is itself a rich anthology of stories. The great

Canadian literary critic Northrop Frye (speaking here not as a Christian, but as a teacher of literature) said of the Bible that:

> It should be taught so early and so thoroughly that it sinks straight to the bottom of the mind, where everything that comes along later can settle on it . . . in the particular context in which I'm speaking now, it's the total shape and structure of the Bible which is most important: the fact that it's a continuous narrative beginning with the Creation and ending with the Last Judgment, and surveying the whole history of mankind, under the symbolic names of Adam and Israel, in between.

It is a story, Christians believe, told by a God who is both "transcendent"—outside the story as authors are outside their books—and "immanent"—hidden at the heart of every story, the Word or "Telling" without which "no thing was made that has been made" (John 1:3).

This transcendent God that we know as the Creator of the great ongoing story of earth and time is, himself, part of that story and has made us part of his story. In the book of scripture God gives us a key to the meaning of the story we glimpse in Creation. It begins with a good purpose ("and God saw all that he had made and it was good"), and goes on to tell of both the joy and pain that come to a world which is allowed to *be* and *do* in freedom. This story consummates in a "Eucatastrophe" (Tolkien invented the word, meaning "a good, grand ending") with the "glory and honor of the nations" (Revelation 21:26) brought together, restored, in the Holy City of God, the New Jerusalem.

We want stories to have happy endings; we hope that our own story will have such an ending. We glimpse that possibility in the very regularity of creation, which tells of One who, in Paul's words to devout pagans, ". . . has shown kindness by giving you rain from heaven and crops in their seasons; he provides you with plenty of food and fills your hearts with joy" (Acts 14: 17). G. K. Chesterton, describing his own growing realization that the world is more than a disconnected collection of facts, writes:

> . . . I had always believed that the world involved magic: now I thought that perhaps it involved a magician. And this pointed [to] a profound emotion always present and sub-conscious; that this world of ours has some purpose; and if there is a purpose, there is a person. I had always felt life first as a story: and if there is a story there is a story-teller.

We and our stories are in danger of losing this sense of "magic," of a large, meaning-giving Story permeating our daily stories, which can often seem meaning*less*. Yet the kingdom of God is about restoration: it is not about some final cataclysmic fix-it so much as it is about God's continual work in restoring meaning to our individual stories. And just as Jesus did not preach without using stories, so God has told us his pattern of restoration in Story.

We were made in God's image: it is our spiritual "genetic code." Though we (and consequently that image) are warped and wounded, in our telling of stories we are trying to remind ourselves of what it means to be made in the image of God, to be part of his story. And our storying is part of that creating and restoring image of God. So, as Northrop Frye's books have helped us understand (see **Helps Along the Way to Good Books for Children**), the Bible is "the Great Code" of Story for *restoring* and *restorying* our lives and our stories.

Franz Kafka defines a book as an "ice-ax to break the seas frozen in our souls." We need the "ice-ax" of story to see pattern, to see meaning, to point out the lack of pattern and meaning in our lives. We need story to discover who we ourselves are and who God is. Stories can bring our fractured lives together, and in doing so they hint at the restoring shape of the great story. Stories can seep into the cracks that have opened up within ourselves and glue us back together.

So, we need to *restore* our children by *restorying* them. In Gary Schmidt's THE SIN EATER, young Cole and his grandfather ponder this place of story in human life:

> "No story ever repeats, Cole," said Grandpa.
> "Then why bother remembering any of them?"
> Grandpa looked right at me. "So we can know who we are. So we can share one another's lives, and somehow carry one another's lives. So we know how to live."
> "Or how not to live," I said softly and left for bed. I slept in thickened darkness without moving all night.

Cole has been the victim of the hard facts essential to some good stories, but his grandfather's insight is profound: we need story to "know how to live."

We need to *restory* our children, not only with the Bible stories (as Deuteronomy 8-11 tells us), but also with all those "bits, dainty and undainty" which, as Tolkien reminds us, human minds and hearts have put into the ancient soup-cauldron of the stories we tell. For these sub-creations of The Story give us hints and clues for the how-to of living wholly or holy (the words have the same root) in a creation that is groaning for wholeness and completion.

When we have given our children good books—that marvelous, restoring food drawn from the centuries-old cauldron of story—will they be able to live life more easily? Will they be happier? Will they have all the Answers? No. We may even make life harder for them—and for us. They will see more and feel more. They will love more and suffer more. They will also care more. They may not necessarily be better Christians. But as Henry Zylstra (himself a fine teacher of stories and The Story) might have put it, there will be more of them to be Christian *with*.

The goal of storytellers . . . consists of fostering in the child . . . compassion and humaneness—this miraculous ability of man to be disturbed by another being's misfortunes, to feel joy about another being's happiness, to experience another's fate as one's own.

—Kornei Chukovsky
Father of Russian Literature for Children

It is my belief that there is no "parents' aid" which can compare with the book in its capacity to establish and maintain a relationship with a child. Its effects extend far beyond the covers of the actual book, and invade every aspect of life . . . .

Because by their very nature they are rooted in language, and because language is essential to human communication, and communication is the life blood of relationships, books *matter.*

—Dorothy Butler

2

Introducing Young Children to Books

❧

Setting the Stage

Reading to babies and young children involves more than just sticking a book in their hands. Even before they are able to grasp a book (or rip out a page or slobber on a corner . . .) the preparations can be made. They are as simple as this:

Read for Yourself
Enjoy Your Kids Now
Accept the Reality of Messiness
Don't Despair over Destroyed Books
Incorporate Books into Everyday Life
No Television (or Videos—even "Christian" Ones!)
Go to the Library

Read for Yourself

Children are very imitative and quickly pick up on the activities that we enjoy. Reading for your own pleasure is an enjoyable way of providing an example. Reading about reading to children can be an inspiration and a help, particularly HONEY FOR A CHILD'S HEART by Gladys Hunt and BABIES NEED BOOKS by Dorothy Butler (see "Helpful Books and Articles" in **Helps Along the Way to Good Books for Children** for a more complete list). Reading for yourself can provide not only an escape from the (sometimes grim) reality of small children but also a chance to gain perspective, energy, and sympathy.

Enjoy Your Kids Now

Sitting and reading a book with a child cuddled up on your lap is a wonderful way to focus both child and parent energies on something positive. It can be the epitome of coziness *or*, depending on the mood, a bouncy time for releasing wiggles.

Accept the Reality of Messiness

If books, games, walks and playing together have priority over dishes, "personal time," laundry, and cleaning, then you *will* have to cope with a messy home (unless you are a miracle worker). Looking at the big, life-sized picture can make it easier to drop the laundry and pick up the book. Studies have shown that children who are played with, stimulated, and touched have bigger brains!

Don't Despair over Destroyed Books

Books are for chewing on, climbing on, and pulling off shelves. Writing some books off as learner books—such as board books and PAT THE BUNNY—makes it easier to deal with the rips, bites, bends, and creases. After all, babies have to *learn* the motor skills of opening a book and turning the pages. Some books (in the crib and bedroom) should be hands-on books. The beautiful books should be kept for when they can be explored under supervision—and for when the children have learned basic "book etiquette."

Incorporate Books into Everyday Life

Books can become part of everyday life, and they can make the mundanity of everyday life exciting. Acting out familiar stories with stuffed animals and toys around your house is a fun way of starting imaginative play. Connecting books and stories to the themes and fixations in a child's life can make both the story *and reality* more memorable. For example, we know a child whose parents came home and read OWL MOON after seeing an owl during a snowy walk. Christmas is a perfect time for connecting stories with The Story and with the excitement of the season.

No Television (or Videos—Even "Christian" Ones!)

Not having this mind-numbing, attention-span-shrinking tool in your home is *crucial* to creating a welcoming atmosphere for books. For more information on the seriousness and validity of this statement, read THE DISAPPEARANCE OF CHILDHOOD by Neil Postman, THE PLUG-IN DRUG by Marie Winn, or FOUR ARGUMENTS FOR THE ELIMINATION OF TELEVISION by Jerry Mander.

Go to the Library

Going to the library is one of the few free indoor "outings" possible for parents of young children. Libraries usually have shelves full of baby board books for teething on! Libraries are also a good source for books which might already be out of print, as well as a cheap way of trying out books you might eventually want to buy.

How to Start

Now the fun begins! Children learn in different ways, so it is important to approach reading from as many angles as possible.

Rhymes

Memorizing nursery rhymes and reciting them to children as they are cared for is a good way to introduce them to the rhythm and texture of words, even before they are aware of their meaning.

Music and Song

Lots of children will listen to singing before they will pay attention to spoken words. Children are very forgiving listeners and, in addition to songs, love to hear regular books and rhymes set to music. Lots of children's tapes have songs from traditional nursery rhymes to give you ideas.

Images

As babies learn to focus they like primary colours and the strong contrasts of black and white. They prefer bright, clear images to soft and fuzzy ones. They also enjoy photos of babies. One of the best sources is THE BABY'S BOOK OF BABIES, photos by Anthea Sieveking. Another great source is your own family photo albums, particularly the baby pictures, perhaps because children can key into the importance of something if they see themselves in it.

Images and Words Together

Look for short books with few words: one picture per idea per page. Repetition is something to look for as well as a sense of story. First books shouldn't be *lessons* in colours, shapes and sizes, but rather they should hint at the wonderful combination of words, rhythm, picture, character, and sequence that make up a book.

❧

A Sample Day

Now that you've set the stage for books and *have started introducing your children to the various aspects of reading, what does an actual day with books look like? We all know that days have certain rhythms (and a book you can read first thing in the morning is often one that will be ignored in that horrible hour before dinner), so here are some suggestions:*

Stretch

Try a few books that will stretch a child's attention, but only at the appropriate time (perhaps in the morning or after a nap, when minds are fresh and ready for something new).

WHEN I WAS YOUNG IN THE MOUNTAINS. Cynthia Rylant.
THE TALE OF MR. JEREMY FISHER. Beatrix Potter.
MAKE WAY FOR DUCKLINGS. Robert McCloskey.
MIKE MULLIGAN AND HIS STEAM SHOVEL. THE LITTLE
    HOUSE. Virginia Lee Burton.
LITTLE OH. Laura Krauss Melmed.

Spontaneous Standards

It is good to have books throughout the day that are everyone's favourites—the kind that you might be able to read in your sleep.

NUTSHELL LIBRARY. WHERE THE WILD THINGS ARE. and IN
    THE NIGHT KITCHEN. Maurice Sendak.
THE LITTLE FUR FAMILY. Margaret Wise Brown.
RHYMES FOR ANNIE ROSE. THE NURSERY COLLECTION.
    OUT AND ABOUT. Shirley Hughes.
JOURNEY CAKE, HO! Ruth Sawyer.
JESSE BEAR, WHAT WILL YOU WEAR? Nancy White Carlstrom.
SOMETHING FROM NOTHING. Phoebe Gilman.
CAPS FOR SALE. Esphyr Slobodkina.

Survival

There are times of the day when you need bounce and rhythm to survive.

SHEEP IN A JEEP and SHEEP IN A SHOP. Nancy Shaw.

JAMBERRY. Bruce Degan.
WE'RE GOING ON A BEAR HUNT. Michael Rosen.
GREEN EGGS AND HAM and THE CAT IN THE HAT COMES BACK.
Dr. Seuss.
DRUMMER HOFF. Barbara Emberley.
JILLIAN JIGGS and THE WONDERFUL PIGS OF JILLIAN JIGGS.
Phoebe Gilman.

Storytelling

Learn to *tell* stories for all those times when reading a book is not possible (toilet times, car trips, line-ups, etc.). Reading and memorizing the general shape of a folk tale or Bible story can give you a vehicle for your own personalized story—as long or as short, as soothing or as wild as you want.

THE THREE BEARS. Illustrated by Feodor Rojankovsky.
THE THREE BILLY GOATS GRUFF. Paul Galdone.
LITTLE RED RIDING HOOD. Illustrated by either Paul Galdone *or*
Feodor Rojankovsky.
Other fairy tales.
"Jesus Stories" (miracles, Christmas) and "God Stories" (creation, prophets).

Scripture

Our faith is the most important inheritance we can give our children. Stories from the Bible, either read or told, are great ways to introduce Christianity to kids before Sunday School packages up each story with a moral lesson, a craft, and a snack.

READ-ALOUD BIBLE STORIES (VOLUMES 1-4). Ella K. Lindvall.
(Volume 3 is our favourite!)
STORIES JESUS TOLD. Nick Butterworth and Mick Inkpen.
THE RHYME BIBLE. L. J. Sattgast.
THE CREATION. James Weldon Johnson.
NOAH'S ARK. Peter Spier.
TOMIE DE PAOLA'S BOOK OF BIBLE STORIES.

BIBLE STORIES FOR CHILDREN.
THE BIBLE!

Sleep

If you miss all the other chances to share stories and books during a day, before bed is the time to set things right. A cozy book or two should be as essential to nighttime routine as brushing teeth. "Sweet dreams, my darling, sleep well, goodnight!"

GOODNIGHT MOON. THE RUNAWAY BUNNY. and LITTLE
    DONKEY, CLOSE YOUR EYES. Margaret Wise Brown.
TIME FOR BED. Mem Fox. (Source of "Sweet Dreams" quote above.)
IF ONCE YOU HAVE SLEPT ON AN ISLAND. Rachel Field.
TEN IN THE BED and TEN OUT OF BED. Penny Dale.
WHEN THE SUN ROSE. Barbara Berger.
THE MIDNIGHT FARM. Reeve Lindbergh.
OWL MOON. Jane Yolen.
THE MAGGIE B. Irene Haas.

See **Helps Along the Way to Good Books for Children** for more suggestions and ideas for reading to and with older children.

This is the sort of book we like
(For you and I are very small)
With pictures stuck in anyhow
And hardly any words at all.

You will not understand a word
Of all the words, including mine;
Never you trouble; you can see—
And all directness is divine.

Stand up and keep your childishness.
Read all the pedants' screeds and strictures.
But don't believe in anything
That can't be told in coloured pictures.

—G. K. Chesterton

3

Picture Books

A perfect picture book is one in which the words and pictures enhance, amplify, and even perhaps tease each other without contradiction or competition. When children are old enough, or at least careful enough, a stack of picture books for them to reverently explore will open up whole new worlds. In the familiar books the pictures will remind them of the words, and in the new books the pictures will help them tell their own stories until they can find an adult reader.

The categories in this section are an effort to bring some sort of direction and order into what would otherwise be a huge, unwieldy amalgam of the amazing and wonderful diversity of the picture book. Some (most!) of these books do *not* fit neatly into any slot, so be sure to see each category as a window to a world rather than as a door to a closet. For instance, Joosse's book MAMA, DO YOU LOVE ME? is under "Family Caring and Nurture" but could as well fit in "Playing Around with Words" or "A Child's Life." Within each section, the order indicates a general increase in complexity, demanding a more mature "hearer." ("Picture Books of Bible Stories" and "Christmas Stories" are in **Bible Stories**).

We have not (but for a few exceptions) included "Easy Readers," which are written mainly for the purpose of teaching kids to read. Familiar picture books are some of the best beginning readers because of the picture cues, the often familiar or possibly memorized text, and the excellent choice of words (as opposed to the excessively tedious selection found in "Easy Readers"). Children learn to read in so many different ways and at different stages of development; "Easy Readers" are used only for a short time and are *so* obviously a stepping stone to another level that most of them are not worth the time and money.

First Books

Introducing Young Children to Books *describes first books and how to suitably acquaint your child with them. However, the following books are the best first books: they are simple and re-readable. They should be on your nursery shelf with a Mother Goose book and a good song book.*

Brown, Margaret Wise. GOODNIGHT MOON. Illustrated by Clement Hurd. The *best* first book. As his room grows darker, a little bunny says "Goodnight" to his toys, his furniture, and the moon. THE RUNAWAY BUNNY. Also illustrated by Hurd—good basic book on security in love. THE CHICKEN BOOK. Another old favourite illustrated by Garth Williams.

Board books—especially books with photographs of babies (babies are fascinated by other babies, including the one they see in the mirror). During that frustrating (for the parents!) rip and chew stage (by the babies), these books survive (better) and reveal a primary fact of reading—books are where you "see" things. Good libraries have lots of these to give you and baby some stimulating variety.

Risom, Ole. I AM A BUNNY. Illustrated by Richard Scarry. Follow a bunny named Nicholas through the seasons until winter snowfall, when he curls up in his hollow tree and dreams about spring. Simple, short, and soothing: a perfect first book.

Williams, Sue. I WENT WALKING. Illustrated by Julie Vivas. An introduction to colours, animals and the whole adventure of seeing.

de Paola, Tomie. MICE SQUEAK, WE SPEAK. One animal per

page makes its noise, and three children announce at intervals, "But I Speak," "But I Say," and "But I Talk." Bright colours; great for an introduction to animals, noises, and on a deeper level, to a primary difference between animals and people.

Carlstrom, Nancy White. JESSE BEAR, WHAT WILL YOU WEAR? Illustrated By Bruce Degan. A bouncily rhyming story of an energetic bear's day from waking to sleeping.

Goodnight Books

Cozy and familiar for the end of the day, these are books to make going to bed special, not dreadful.

GOODNIGHT MOON. Of course! For description, see first book in "First Books," above.

Fox, Mem. TIME FOR BED. Illustrated by Jane Dyer. As necessary as GOODNIGHT MOON; soothing, repetitive; the pictures are soporific without being too sweet. However, this can be a wild book as well, with buzzing bees and hissing snakes.

Dale, Penny. TEN IN THE BED. The traditional story/song about a wide-awake child pushing his nine stuffed animals out of bed (the animals raid the kitchen for bedtime snacks) until the child calls them back. TEN OUT OF BED. The same child and his nine stuffed animal friends each pick a theme for their play (the circus, airplanes, theatre . . .) until one by one all drop off to sleep. Another excellent (though on a different theme) book by the same author-illustrator: ROSIE AND HER BABIES. A sweet story of a little girl patiently waiting for her mother to finish putting the baby to sleep.

Brown, Margaret Wise. LITTLE DONKEY, CLOSE YOUR EYES. Illustrated by Ashley Wolff. Extremely beautiful drawings look like brightly-coloured woodcuts. Animals in different parts of the world are urged to close their eyes as nearby humans also settle in for the night.

Lindbergh, Reeve. THE MIDNIGHT FARM. Illustrated (wonder-fully) by Susan Jeffers. Another farm book *and* a good night book *and* a counting book. Lindbergh says she wants to "make the nighttime dark-ness less frightening" by describing "the farm where we used to live . . . the animals and their activities at night in as warm and comforting a way as possible."

Sandburg, Carl. THE WEDDING PROCESSION OF THE RAG DOLL AND THE BROOM HANDLE AND WHO WAS IN IT. Illus-trated by Harriet Pincus. From the Musical Soup Eaters to the Sleepy Heads, "It was a grand procession."

Seuss, Dr. SLEEP BOOK. Vintage Seuss—describes all kinds of weird creatures all over the world who are going to sleep. The tally keeps rising, and at the end, "Ninety-nine zillion nine trillion and two / Creatures are sleeping so . . . How about you? When you put out *your* lights / Then the number will be ninety-nine zillion / nine trillion and three."

✿

Playing Around with Words

Read a few of these books and see if you don't find yourself rhyming and bouncing your words—real or imagined—for the sheer fun of it!

MOTHER GOOSE. Illustrated by Tomie de Paola. Simple, visually ac-cessible for young eyes. For lots more Mother Goose, see the "Nurs-ery Rhymes" section in **Poetry**.

Brooke, L. Leslie. JOHNNY CROW'S GARDEN. Funny animal rhymes with simple but hilarious pictures. Good for developing a sense of words and word-play.

Emberley, Barbara. DRUMMER HOFF. Illustrated by Ed Emberley. Adapted from a folk poem. This is a vibrantly illustrated book of successive characters helping to ready a cannon. "Drummer Hoff fires it off" with an explosively-loud, full-page, "KAHBAHBLOOM!!!" The final page's picture of the cannon sitting in a flower-filled meadow and covered with spider's webs and bird's nests will assuage any pacifistic pangs of guilt over this Caldecott Medal book.

Shaw, Nancy. SHEEP IN A JEEP[...SHIP...SHOP]. Illustrated by Margot Apple. One of several sheep...eep[...ip...op] books that delight in words and some rather fantastic sheep shenanigans.

Degan, Bruce. JAMBERRY. A rollicking, rhyming story about a bear, a boy and a bunch of berries.

Gag, Wanda. MILLIONS OF CATS. A compassionate couple find themselves sheltering "millions and billions and trillions of cats."

Seuss, Dr. GREEN EGGS AND HAM. THE CAT IN THE HAT COMES BACK. Etc! Dr. Seuss fosters a love of words real and imagined!

Rosen, Michael. WE'RE GOING ON A BEAR HUNT. Illustrated by Helen Oxenbury. A father and his children go out for a walk through grass ("swishy swashy"), a river ("splash splosh"), etc. . . . until they meet a bear in a cave and hurry home again through all those places in reverse. Repetitive and fun.

Sawyer, Ruth. JOURNEY CAKE, HO! Illustrated by Robert McCloskey. Johnny the bound-out boy is forced to leave the farm (after disaster strikes) with only a big Journey Cake to accompany him. When the cake drops out of his pack, it leads Johnny and many greedy farm animals on a circuitous route back home!

Bannatyne-Cugnet, Jo. A PRAIRIE ALPHABET. Illustrated by Yvette Moore. An alphabet book with wonderful rhythm and beautiful pictures (definitely visual feasts!). The pictures are as full of detail as the text is full of alliteration.

Dodds, Dayle. SING SOPHIE. Illustrated by Rosanne Litzinger. Sophie is a cowgirl with a song in her heart that needs to come out, but no one in her family will let her sing until . . . ! The illustrations are silly, almost cartoon style, and the word choice is corny and delightfully catchy.

Day, Alexandra. FRANK AND ERNEST. These two friends, a bear and an elephant, take on the operation of "Sally's Diner" for a few days and give quite fantastic names to the rather ordinary food. Good fun with word pictures.

A Child's Life

The constants which make up a child's life—messy rooms, creative play, mud puddles, favourite colours, special dolls, and bad days—are celebrated in these books.

Ahlberg, Janet and Allan. THE BABY'S CATALOGUE. Contents include sections on Mornings, High Chairs and Breakfasts; Accidents; Teas and Books; and Baths and Bedtimes—a catalogue of everyday life that we all recognize as real. See other good books by this husband-wife team, such as EACH PEACH PEAR PLUM.

Hughes, Shirley. DOGGER. And many others. Cozy stories and poems with delightfully homey and familiar characters in British middle-class neighbourhood settings. These books are reassuringly solid and dependable.

Stinson, Kathy. RED IS BEST. Illustrated by Robin Baird Lewis. A whole-hearted, 100%-prejudiced, closed-minded case for the superior-ity of RED.

Gilman, Phoebe. JILLIAN JIGGS. THE WONDERFUL PIGS OF JILLIAN JIGGS. JILLIAN JIGGS TO THE RESCUE. Rhyming stories about a very creative girl who, in the first book, thwarts her mother's orders to clean her room by indulging in grand imaginary play. In the second, she spends a day in a creative frenzy making pigs (directions for how to make your own pigs are in the back of the book). In the third, she and her friends capture a 'monster' with their monster machine.

Haas, Irene. THE MAGGIE B. Margaret Barnstable wishes for a day on a sailing ship named after her. Her wish comes true, and her wonderfully illustrated perfect day (complete with storm) will inspire many an imaginary journey.

Viorst, Judith. ALEXANDER AND THE TERRIBLE, HORRIBLE, NO-GOOD, VERY BAD DAY. A basic lesson of life: "Some days are like that—even in Australia."

Segal, Lore. TELL ME A MITZI. Illustrated by Harriet Pincus. Three stories of the mutual caregiving that is part of family life. These humorous stories are great examples of how parents can make up simple repetetive stories from everyday life: having a cold, going to visit Grandma and Grandpa, and going for a walk. The 70's-style illustrations are of plain, pudgy people in pretty plaid pants patterns.

Nivola, Claire. ELISABETH. The true story of Ruth, a girl who *loves* her doll Elisabeth. They are inseparable until the family is forced to flee Nazi Germany and leave everything, including Elisabeth. Ruth immigrates to the United States, grows up, and eventually has a daughter who wants a doll for her birthday . . .

Cooney, Barbara (Illustrator). Barbara Cooney is the illustrator for several books which speak to the longings of all children: for play— ROXABOXEN—a story by Alice McLerran about a "real" pretend town built and "lived in" by her great-aunt; for friendship—EMILY— written by Michael Bedard about a child's recluse friend, the poet Emily Dickinson; for family—ONLY OPAL: THE DIARY OF A

YOUNG GIRL—taken from the journal of an orphan pioneer girl, Opal Whiteley; for acceptance—BASKET MOON—in this story by Mary Lyn Ray, a boy learns about rejection *and* about the gift of support from friends; and for longing to know what you're going to be when you grow up—HATTIE AND THE WILD WAVES.

Carrier, Roch. THE HOCKEY SWEATER. Illustrated by Sheldon Cohen. A Canadian Classic about a boy for whom, as for many boys, hockey is the be-all and end-all of life—and a hockey sweater the symbol of all.

✿

Family Caring and Nurture

We need books that show us what family love is like (or should be like) day after day, year after year, and generation after generation.

Brown, Margaret Wise. THE LITTLE FUR FAMILY. Illustrated by Garth Williams. A small book—with a fuzzy, furry cover—about a cozy fur family. Falling asleep over a book has never been so comfortable.

Joosse, Barbara M. MAMA, DO YOU LOVE ME? Illustrated by Barbara Lavallee. The answer, over and over again, is Yes—no matter what. An Inuit setting—both in imagery and in casting of mother and daughter.

Johnston, Tony. YONDER. Illustrated by Lloyd Bloom. A young couple goes to a valley, plants a tree, builds a home—and eventually their children (and their grandchildren) bury the much-loved grandfather under the old apple tree they had planted.

Rylant, Cynthia. THE RELATIVES CAME. Illustrated by Stephen Gammell. Captures all the chaos and comfort of visits from cousins and uncles and aunts. APPALACHIA. Illustrated by Barry Moser. A pictured record of the patterns of life in a mountain community that reminds us of the basic good of life. The same theme, only in a format that is better for young children, is in WHEN I WAS YOUNG

IN THE MOUNTAINS, illustrated by Diane Goode (these books should however not be seen as alternates; APPALACHIA is Moser at his finest in depicting meaning and character).

Loh, Morag. TUCKING MOMMY IN. Illustrated by Donna Rawlins. Two daughters cooperate to put a tired mommy to bed—parenting come full circle, as it does.

Williams, Vera. A CHAIR FOR MY MOTHER. A little girl saves her money to finally buy a comfortable chair for her hardworking mother. A warm, good story of the patient steadfastness of caring.

Gray, Libba Moore. MY MAMA HAD A DANCING HEART. Illustrated by Raúl Colón. A story with a "tip-tapping, song-singing, finger-snapping" rhythm that celebrates seasons, traditions, dancing, and mothers and daughters.

Springstubb, Tricia. MY MINNIE IS A JEWEL. Illustrated by Jim LaMarche. Some would call this book sexist—and maybe that is why it's out of print. But it is a hilarious reminder of the marital verities of trust and loyalty. Minnie is *always* Henry's jewel—no matter what culinary disaster he has to swallow when he gets home.

Ross, Lillian Hammer. BUBA LEAH AND HER PAPER CHILDREN. Illustrated by Mary Morgan. Through the years, Buba Leah writes letters to her family who have left her behind in the old country—to her paper children. A poignant story of separation from loved ones who, in this story, are happily reunited in the end when the paper children send Buba money to come to them.

Greenfield, Eloise. GRANDPA'S FACE. Illustrated by Floyd Cooper. A child learns that no matter what her actor grandpa looks like, he *always* loves her.

Melmed, Laura Krauss. THE RAINBABIES. Gorgeously illustrated by Jim LaMarche. Another book about faithfulness—an older couple show such steadfast and courageous love for their miniature, foundling rainbabies that they are given a child of their own. LITTLE

OH. Also illustrated by Jim LaMarche. Very much the same theme, but in this book a woman's love for her origami child brings to her a family of her own. These books are rich, moving stories of the selfless love at the core of marriage and family.

MacLachlan, Patricia. ALL THE PLACES TO LOVE. Illustrated by Mike Wimmer. A *great* book that goes right to the heart of what it *should* mean to be born into a family and thereby given both love and *place*.

Cooney, Barbara. ISLAND BOY. Based on the true history of a family's settlement of an island off the coast of New England. The youngest son grows up, goes away to sea, and comes back to raise a family—and finally to die—on the island of his boyhood.

Oberman, Sheldon. THE ALWAYS PRAYER SHAWL. Illustrated by Ted Lewin. Tradition is carried along through the years by the handing down, from generation to generation, of a prayer shawl—which *always* is worn for prayer and *always* is a reminder of the great unchanging heritage of love between grandfather and grandson, and which survives changes of time, place and people: "Some things change, and some things don't change."

Wells, Rosemary. WAITING FOR THE EVENING STAR. Illustrated by Susan Jeffers. A family story underlining the importance of stability, depth—rather than breadth—in experience, and the durable meaning of *place*, but also acknowledging the fact that in the same family some members are *not* content with life on the farm and *need* to leave.

❧

Creation and Seeing

On the subject of Creation (often called 'Environmental Awareness') there are three winners in the Have-A-Message-But-Still-Worth-Reading category:

Dr. Seuss. THE LORAX.
Peet, Bill. THE WUMP WORLD.
Van Allsburg, Chris. JUST A DREAM.

The other books in this section help make children aware of Creation by filling them with great love for all that is beautiful, instead of great fear for all that has gone wrong. Seeing the beauty of the world around us means also being made aware of the cycles of life: birth and death, the seasons, etc.

Carle, Eric. THE VERY HUNGRY CATERPILLAR. A simple story of a hungry caterpillar teaches metamorphosis, counting, colours, numbers, days of the week, and the names of basic fruits. *Plus*, children enjoy putting their fingers into the hole it makes as it eats its way through the book! A HOUSE FOR HERMIT CRAB. In his effort to decorate his house, this crab introduces us to intertidal sealife— and to loyalty, sacrifice and friendship.

Berger, Barbara. GRANDFATHER TWILIGHT. The tones of twilight are illuminated in this exquisitely illustrated fantasy about an old man in the forest who every evening gives a pearl to the "silence above the sea." This book captures the ethereal interplay of day, dusk and darkness.

Keats, Ezra Jack. THE SNOWY DAY. A classic story of a little boy's discovery of the wonder of snow.

Brett, Jan. THE MITTEN. A number of animals find shelter in a mitten. ANNIE AND THE WILD ANIMALS. A variation of THE MITTEN (both have a wonderful substory in the margins—a hallmark of Brett's illustrations).

Shulevitz, Uri. RAIN RAIN RIVERS. Rain drops on people and houses, descends on streets and towns, turns into rivers, and eventually makes its way to the sea.

Heller, Ruth. CHICKENS AREN'T THE ONLY ONES. A brilliantly illustrated rhyming book about the animals who lay eggs.

Fyleman, Rose. A FAIRY WENT A-MARKETING. Illustrated by Jamichael Henterly. A sprightly poem with ethereal illustrations about a fairy purchasing, enjoying, and then releasing fellow flora and fauna.

Ziefert, Harriet. A NEW COAT FOR ANNA. Illustrated by Anita Lobel. A girl and her mother in post-war Europe exercise great patience, ingenuity, and bartering skills as they start with sheep and end with a beautiful new red coat for Anna. (A variation of PELLE'S NEW SUIT.)

Wells, Rosemary. FOREST OF DREAMS. Illustrated by Susan Jeffers. This gem of words and paintings glories in God's gifts of hands, ears, strength—all we have with which to enjoy the unfolding seasons of creation.

Beskow, Elsa. PELLE'S NEW SUIT. A woolen suit—from sheep—through spinning, dyeing and sewing. CHILDREN OF THE FOR-EST. A *little* (mushroom-sized) forest family lives "off the land" and helps us see and know the intricacies of the life of a forest.

Sheldon, Dyan. THE WHALES' SONG. Illustrated by Gary Blythe. A young girl learns to listen for the singing of whales. The "listen-ing" here goes beyond hearing sounds—in a joyful responsive-ness to the richness of creation, caught beautifully by the paint-ings of Blythe.

Cooney, Barbara. MISS RUMPHIUS. Based on the true story of another New Englander, "the lupine lady," a woman who loved lupine, and planted it everywhere. THE OX-CART MAN. Illustrated by Cooney. Written by Donald Hall. A pioneer family lives a long way from town—but all year they grow and make things to trade, which the father takes to market on his ox-cart.

Yolen, Jane. OWL MOON. Illustrated by John Schoenherr. A gentle and deeply good story about fathering, owls and the night. HONKERS. Illustrated by Leslie Baker. A simple yet rich interplay of love and loneliness, waiting and leave taking, goose eggs and family life.

Rylant, Cynthia. THE DREAMER. Illustrated by Barry Moser. A surprising story about the beginning of art and the world.

Ryder, Joanne. THE WATERFALL'S GIFT. Illustrated by Richard Jesse Watson. A young girl visits her grandfather's cabin in the North Woods and discovers treasures hidden in its deepest places.

Parnall, Peter. APPLE TREE. Any books illustrated by Peter Parnall (sometimes others do the writing) are worth careful attention for their attentiveness to and delight in the detail of creation. This one is about the life in an apple tree through the seasons. (See the "Issues/Aging" section for another—ANNIE AND THE OLD ONE.)

Van Allsburg, Chris. TWO BAD ANTS. Adventures in the world strictly from an ant's viewpoint. Excellent in teaching respect for perspective!

Myers, Christopher and Lynne Born. MCCREPHY'S FIELD. Mr. McCrephy leaves his Ohio farm to go out west, and he returns 50 years later an old man. The book describes how his farm slowly changes from neatly tilled fields to a woods (with trees higher than the barn) supporting deer, opposums, and other wild life.

McCloskey, Robert. TIME OF WONDER. Summer on an island in Maine, described with awe and joy at the wonder of fiddlehead ferns, old stones, tides, quiet mornings, storms, "and one pair of eyes watching over all."

Hughes, Monica. A HANDFUL OF SEEDS. Illustrated by Luis Garay. A gently- and beautifully-done story of stewardship of God's gifts in creation—in this case, seeds to be planted and nurtured in a city vacant-lot garden of Central America. Avoids the threatening urgency often found in environmentalist books for children.

Climo, Lindee. CHESTER'S BARN. Detailed life in a Prince Edward Island farm yard and barn, illustrated with homey farm animal pictures in warm brown tones.

Friendship

Friendship can encompass much more than "my best friend in my class at school." Most of the books in this section are about unusual friendships and the loyal love or sense of fun which they entail.

de Regniers, Beatrice Schenk. MAY I BRING A FRIEND? A little boy invites his friends from the zoo (one by one) to share his tea with the King and the Queen.

Isadora, Rachel. BEN'S TRUMPET. Ben's imaginary trumpet is his only companion—and he plays it with all his heart and soul. Finally a jazz trumpeter hears his "music" and reaches out to him with love— and lessons!

Wahl, Jan. DOCTOR RABBIT. Illustrated by Peter Parnall. Very good pictures and story about a rabbit who helps other animals with such dedication that he gets sick from exhaustion and must then be nurtured by them.

Seuss, Dr. THIDWICK, THE BIG-HEARTED MOOSE. One of many extremely creative books by this author, exploring the dangers of being *too* hospitable (or, as they say these days, "not having proper boundaries").

Geringer, Laura. A THREE-HAT DAY. Illustrated by Arnold Lobel. A man with a passion for hats finally finds a kindred spirit—a woman with a wild love for . . . hats.

Wild, Margaret and Dee Huxley. MR. NICK'S KNITTING. Another book on friendship which is not only fun, but also subtly shows how to care for a friend who is sick.

Stewart, Sarah. THE GARDENER. Illustrated by David Small. Lydia Grace Finch, sent to live with her uncle (a baker) in New York City, brings to life the "Bloom where you're planted" saying as she fills the tenement building with flowers and makes friends with Uncle Jim, his employees, and the cat. The story is told in the form of letters.

Visual Feasts

Some picture books (particularly redone fairy tales) have gorgeous detailed illustrations but long, overly detailed texts. These actually seem to be geared toward an adult market. However, the books in this section, though sometimes quite detailed and beautiful, are books for gazing at by both adults and children.

Spier, Peter. NOAH'S ARK. A terse, yet theologically rich, old Dutch poem precedes a picture-telling of the Bible story, complete with the inevitable crowding and chaos of all those "two-by-twos." JONAH. Includes a map and historical background. PEOPLE. Pictures all our shapes and sizes, habitats and hobbies. Some words in this book, but the half-pages of all those noses and eyes are mainly about the fun of *seeing*, in which Spier delights. RAIN and CHRISTMAS. More picture-tellings. CLOUDS. "What does it look like?"—imagination and cloud-shapes. BORED—NOTHING TO DO! Two bored boys take sheets, the baby buggy, the car—and other family belongings—to create a real, working (for a bit) airplane. *But*, after they put all the stolen parts of their contraption away (by their mother's order), they again complain that they are bored—nothing to do.

Dillon, Leo and Diane. TO EVERY THING THERE IS A SEASON. All 15 phrases in this excerpt from Ecclesiastes are illustrated in different styles, including an Egyptian tomb mural, a European woodcut, a Greek classic vase painting, a Russian icon, and an example of stone-cut Inuit art.

Locker, Thomas. WHERE THE RIVER BEGINS. SAILING WITH THE WIND. THE BOY WHO HELD BACK THE SEA. Locker's books give us a love for landscape reminiscent of Constable and Turner, yet richly grounded in the "inscape" of human character.

Wiesner, David. TUESDAY. Caldecott Medal Winner for 1991, this nearly wordless book, in the spirit of Van Allsburg, reveals a night-time invasion of a town by frogs on lily-pad magic carpets—What If?!

Van Allsburg, Chris. THE MYSTERIES OF HARRIS BURDICK. THE GARDEN OF ABDUL GASAZI. BEN'S DREAM. JUMANJI. THE POLAR EXPRESS. (a "Santa" book). Beautiful, eerie books in which the "other" world keeps breaking into the "real" world.

Collington, Peter. THE ANGEL AND THE SOLDIER BOY. No words, but plenty of action as the toys of a little girl come alive while she sleeps.

❧

History and a Sense of Place

Fiction can portray the essence of a place or a time more than an encyclopedia article or an educational book. Fiction is also more palatable! Finding books that give a strong sense of where one lives is important for creating a local mythology and realizing the value in one's own geographical place.

In a time when there is much uprooting of families and frequent global travel, it is good to keep in touch with roots (both historical and situational). You may have to search locally for books about your roots and place, and you may (if you are a mobile family) have to decide where that place is.

Included in this section are several books that are particular to our place: the west coast of Canada, where our roots are nourished by coastal waters, long grey winter days of rain and mist, the sight of orca whales, and the sound of fog horns.

Perry, Robert. THE FERRYBOAT RIDE. Illustrated by Greta Guzek. A poem full of British Columbian ferry boat sights and sounds, rhymes and rhythms—even has Active Pass and (*we* think) Galiano Island.

Hedderwick, Mairi. KATIE MORAG'S ISLAND STORIES. THE BIG KATIE MORAG STORYBOOK. The setting is island life—whether that be in the Scottish Hebrides or the Gulf Islands—and the stories ring true not only to island life, but also to any child's love of the seashore.

Alderson, Sue. IDA AND THE WOOL SMUGGLERS. Illustrated by Ann Blades. Everyone thinks Ida is too young to help with the sheep run and too young to hold a baby, until she saves Tandy and her lambs from the wool smugglers. This book is set on the Gulf Islands and the pictures have a definite west coast touch.

Waterton, Betty. A SALMON FOR SIMON. PETTRANELLA. Illustrated by Ann Blades. Rich synchronization of text and art in stories that capture Canadian experience: a boy on a beach enthralled with a salmon; an immigrant girl struggling to bring her past and present together with flower seeds from her grandmother.

Blades, Ann. MARY OF MILE 18. THE COTTAGE AT CRESCENT BEACH. Beautiful evocations of place and mood in good stories with specific British Columbian settings.

Rand, Gloria. BABY IN A BASKET. Pictures by Ted Rand. Based on a true story of a journey through the Alaska wilderness in 1917, this is an adventure complete with a sleigh ride, a lost baby in a basket, and a river accident. A bit scary for young children, but it does have a satisfying conclusion.

Reynolds, Marilynn. BELLE'S JOURNEY. Illustrated by Stephen McCallum. Based on a true story of winter on the Canadian prairies—a girl and her horse survive a storm.

Wild, Margaret. LET THE CELEBRATIONS BEGIN! Illustrated by Julie Vivas. A true story of the greatness and courageous hopefulness of the human spirit—about the women of the Belsen concentration camp who made toys from their own ragged clothes for the children to celebrate the longed-for liberation.

Kurelek, William. A PRAIRIE BOY'S WINTER. A PRAIRIE BOY'S SUMMER. LUMBERJACK. Kurelek is an artist, an immigrant from the Ukraine (a number of his books portray the immigrant experience in Canada), and a Christian.

D'Aulaire, Ingri and Edgar Parin. OLA. CHILDREN OF THE NORTHERN LIGHTS. ABRAHAM LINCOLN. GEORGE WASHINGTON. POCAHONTAS. Carefully-researched, -written, and -illustrated stories of other lands and other people—a beautiful synchrony of words and pictures.

Holling, Holling Clancy. PADDLE TO THE SEA. A toy canoe made by an Indian boy goes with the snow-melt down through the Great Lakes, out the St. Lawrence, to the ocean. We learn geography and history as we follow its progress. TREE IN THE TRAIL. SEABIRD. MINN OF THE MISSISSIPPI. Again, the stories of a tree and a bird and a turtle become vehicles for history.

Folk Tales and Fairy Tales

Vast numbers of illustrated versions of the old tales of human culture continue to be published. In general they should be told aloud, as they were throughout most of history, or at least read from a collection, so children can "dress" the bones of these stories with the fabric of their own needs and longings. But, in an effort to keep the genre alive, here are some suggestions if you want to give children a "foretaste of glory."

Ross, K. K. COZY IN THE WOODS. Illustrated by Jane Dyer. A very good version of the old tale, "Stone Soup."

Galdone, Paul. THE BILLY GOATS GRUFF. A childhood favourite retold as we all remember it: a simple, easy telling for a young listener. Such good basic tellings with accessible illustrations are hard to come by. Try to find equivalent tellings of other old favourites, such as THE THREE LITTLE PIGS (Margot Zemach), THE LITTLE

RED HEN (Galdone), HENNY PENNY (Galdone), and THE GIN-GERBREAD BOY (Galdone).

Rojankovsky, Feodor. THE THREE BEARS. Earthy illustrations with nice furry bears in a folksy cottage setting.

Gilman, Phoebe. SOMETHING FROM NOTHING. A retelling of a fine old Jewish tale in which a little boy's blanket goes through many creative "recyclings." Wonderful sub-story of what a mouse family does with the scraps.

Stevens, Janet. TOPS AND BOTTOMS. Stevens adapted this story from European folk takes and Brer Rabbit stories. She had fun making the illustrations for the book on paper made from garden vegetables and gardening clothes. She also had fun putting it together: the book is read from top to bottom rather than from side to side. A story of wits and industry winning out over wealth and laziness.

Martin, Rafe. THE ROUGH-FACE GIRL. Illustrated by David Shannon. An Algonquin version of Cinderella with this twist: the third sister is scarred and charred and becomes beautiful only through the love of the great Invisible Being. A profoundly Christian story. Also, by the same team: THE BOY WHO LIVED WITH THE SEALS, a Chinook Indian legend in the Celtic tradition of the Selkie (Seal) People.

Dixon, Ann. HOW RAVEN BROUGHT LIGHT TO PEOPLE. Illustrated by James Watts. A telling of the Northwest Coast Raven myth that reveals several striking Biblical parallels.

Brett, Jan. BEAUTY AND THE BEAST. Brett's ability to tell two stories at once illuminates our understanding of this old tale which, though connected with Madame Beaumont, has been told in some guise through the ages as human beings have struggled with the continued discrepancy between outward appearance and inner reality. GOLDILOCKS AND THE THREE BEARS. Brett's illustrations with her characteristic marginal substories enrich our understanding of this old story.

Watson, Richard Jesse. TOM THUMB. A retelling in both word and art that captures the wonder and vulnerability of being only as large as a thumb.

Toye, William. THE LOON'S NECKLACE. Illustrated by Elizabeth Cleaver. The best and most hauntingly beautiful of several books on Canadian mythology by this author-illustrator team.

Hunt, Angela Elwell, reteller. THE TALE OF THREE TREES. Illustrated by Tim Jonke. Three trees dream great dreams of what they want to be. Each tree becomes something quite common and ordinary which in the end turns out to be far and away more glorious than its grandiose dream, for each thing (manger, boat, cross) is part of the life story of Jesus.

Mollel, Tololwa. THE ORPHAN BOY. Illustrated by Paul Morin. The pictures and the words of this legend of the star Venus reveal the rich roots of the story in African Masai tradition.

de Paola, Tomie. THE CLOWN OF GOD. A retelling of a traditional story of an old clown whose joy in life is juggling. de Paola is a name to look for when picking out children's books; his illustrations are simple and clear and the stories he chooses to illustrate are rich and good. He has also written a series of stories of saints: FRANCIS, THE POOR MAN OF ASSISI. PATRICK, PATRON SAINT OF IRELAND. CHRISTOPHER, THE HOLY GIANT.

Grimm, Wilhelm and Jacob. DEAR MILI. Illustrated and retold by Maurice Sendak. A richly woven, deeply moving tale of life and death and the journey of a child between them. In no other book is Sendak's strong hold on the interior life and the exterior shape of the deep truth of the folktale more clearly felt. HANSEL AND GRETEL. SNOW WHITE AND THE SEVEN DWARVES. Illustrated by Susan Jeffers, who captures the mythic richness of these old favourites. LITTLE RED RIDING HOOD. Illustrated by Trina Schart Hyman.

❦

"Glimpses of Glory in Other Worlds": Fantasy and Imagination

These stories and pictures enhance the sense that there is something more than everyday life. They validate children's desire to glorify the everyday and, through fantasy and imagination, to expand their horizons beyond their sometimes limited environment.

Sendak, Maurice. WHERE THE WILD THINGS ARE. A boy's room changes into a forest filled with "wild things." After a wild rumpus, he returns, "in and out of weeks and over a year," to the safety of his own bed and a supper that is still hot! NUTSHELL LIBRARY. Four tiny books in a little case to carry around and *read*. Especially good is CHICKEN SOUP WITH RICE. IN THE NIGHT KITCHEN. A little boy dreams about cooking a morning cake in the Night Kitchen—"Milk in the batter, Milk in the batter/ We bake cake and nothing's the matter." This book is a family favourite; it continues to delight our eyes and ears to the extent that many of the phrases have become refrains.

Berger, Barbara. WHEN THE SUN ROSE. This glowing and beautiful book with roses, butterflies, rainbows, dolls and a cosy lion is a story about the sun and friendship.

Ungerer, Tomi. ZERALDA'S OGRE. The delectable delights of little Zeralda's cuisine change the diet and life of an ogre (and his friends).

Pitman, Helena Clare. ONCE WHEN I WAS SCARED. Illustrated by Ted Rand. A grandfather tells this story to his grandson. Once, when the grandfather was a little boy, he was sent "across two hills and through a dark wood," changing himself into different wild animals for courage to survive the trip.

Browne, Anthony. THE TUNNEL. A little girl goes through a dark tunnel, a dark forest and fears of giants and witches to be able to hug her pesky brother back to life. A mythic story of great love casting out fear. (Be sure to pay special attention to the wall paper!)

Mayer, Mercer. LIZA LOU AND THE YELLER BELLY SWAMP. Liza Lou manages to outwit the devils, gobblygooks, witches, and haunts of the yeller belly swamp. This delight is so well written that by the end the reader will have slipped effortlessly into the appropriate Louisiana drawl.

Spalding, Andrea (of Pender Island, British Columbia). SARAH MAY AND THE NEW RED DRESS. Pictures by Janet Wilson. A girl wants a red dress (more than just a dark one that will last and be cheap and won't show the dirt), and eventually gets her wish with the help of a secret, encouraging friend—the West Wind. IT'S RAINING, IT'S POURING. Illustrated by Leslie Elizabeth Watts. Little Girl travels by ladder up into the rainy cloud country to see why Old Man is snoring. (This Old Man has a cold *in* his head, not a bump *on* it.) She brings a few home remedies, cures him, and barely makes it home before the sun comes out and the clouds disappear.

Willard, Nancy. THE HIGH RISE GLORIOUS SKITTLE SKAT ROARIOUS SKY PIE ANGEL FOOD CAKE. Illustrated by Richard Jesse Watson. A wild and funny adventure with angels and a cake recipe. Angelically beautiful illustrations.

Rylant, Cynthia. AN ANGEL FOR SOLOMON SINGER. Illustrated by Peter Catalanotto. This is a fine book about a lonely homesick man in downtown New York City.

All About Animal Anthropomorphism

(Otherwise known as 'Animals Are People, Too.') Some of these books make the lives of animals more accessible, as in MAKE WAY FOR DUCKLINGS; most, however, use animals as vehicles for pointing out our own human frailties and antics—particularly the Kevin Henkes and Rosemary Wells books.

Dunbar, Joyce. THE VERY SMALL. Creatively illustrated by Debi Gliori. Giant Bear tries to make a "very small something" comfortable in his Big House with his Giant Mommy and Daddy Bear. They share toys, a meal, a bath, and bed until Giant Baby Bear's sneeze sends the Very Small back to his own bed—where *his* own bear suddenly seems very small!

Potter, Beatrix. THE TALE OF PETER RABBIT. THE TALE OF MR. JEREMY FISHER. THE TALE OF SQUIRREL NUTKIN. And many others—"little rabbits cannot afford to spend six shillings on one book" (Beatrix Potter)—so these are *small* (in size, cost, and length) tidbits of literature. Watch out for spin-offs and fakes. The real stories are definite treasures, as are the delightful characters.

McCloskey, Robert. MAKE WAY FOR DUCKLINGS. A classic children's book with quotable text ("Jack, Kack, Lack, Mack, Nack, Ouack, Pack, and Quack"), simple but accurate one-colour drawings, and an acute sense of what is important: a safe place to sleep and free food!

Wells, Rosemary. HAZEL'S AMAZING MOTHER. MAX AND RUBY Series. VOYAGE TO THE BUNNY PLANET Series. In HAZEL'S AMAZING MOTHER, Hazel and Eleanor (her doll) get lost and are beset by bullies until rescued by Hazel's amazing mother. She flies through the air (thereby frightening away the bullies) and brings with her a marvelous picnic. In the MAX AND RUBY series, Max and Ruby are a brother and sister who annoy each other in love, as only siblings can. The VOYAGE TO THE BUNNY PLANET series transports bunny children (who are having *really* bad days) for refreshing visits to the Bunny Planet.

Henkes, Kevin. LILY'S PURPLE PLASTIC PURSE. CHRYSANTHE-MUM. JULIUS: THE BABY OF THE WORLD. OWEN. CHESTER'S WAY. SHEILA RAE. All these are extremely funny stories about mice-people with very familiar problems: unjust treatment from your favourite teacher, a peculiar name, a new baby brother, giving up your security blanket, etc.

Lobel, Arnold. FROG AND TOAD ARE FRIENDS. FROG AND TOAD
ALL YEAR. Homey stories about two friends who put up with
each other's foibles and idiosyncrasies. These are very readable
readers. (Also, the tapes of Arnold Lobel reading these stories are
excellent.)

✿

Plain Old Good Stories

*These are books that are very hard to slot into any category, often be-
cause they bridge so many. Some are stories on the basic childhood theme of
security—where threats to obscurity and unimportance (and what child doesn't
wrestle with that!) don't win over a loyal love that says, "You Matter." Some
are simply great fun. All of them share a basic joy in life.*

Slobodkina, Esphyr. CAPS FOR SALE. A cap salesman wakes up from a
nap under a tree, only to discover that all but one of his caps have
been stolen—by monkeys!

Wood, Audrey. THE NAPPING HOUSE. Everyone is on Gramma's bed
and on Gramma for a nap—including, unfortunately, a flea. KING
BIDGOOD'S IN THE BATHTUB. Hilarious story of a king who
conducts all his business for the day *in* his bathtub—until his page
pulls the plug. Both are illustrated by her husband, Don Wood—
and the page who pulls the plug is their son!

Gliori, Debi. THE SNOW LAMBS. Sam's faith in his beloved Bess the
sheepdog is vindicated when she rescues the best ewe from a wild
snowstorm. The ewe gives birth to two lambs in a safe cosy ending to Bess's harrowing adventure—and to Sam's fears. A simple
story with illustrations showing the parallel experiences of Sam and
Bess.

Brown, Margaret Wise. THE SAILOR DOG. Illustrated by Garth
Williams. Scuppers the Sailor Dog is both sensible and adventur-

ous. Everything from his wardrobe to his shipwreck is just right. (Try reading THE MAGGIE B. next.)

McCloskey, Robert. BLUEBERRIES FOR SAL. Sal and a bear cub lose their mothers and find each other's before returning to their own, all the while picking and eating blueberries on Blueberry Hill. ONE MORNING IN MAINE. Sal's first loose tooth (and its loss) is a major event—almost eclipsing a trip to Buck's harbour in the motor boat. BURT DOW, RIVER BOAT MAN. Burt Dow has a "whale of an adventure." LENTIL. Lentil impresses the entire town with his harmonica playing. Old, reliable favourites.

Burton, Virginia Lee. CALICO THE WONDER HORSE OR THE SAGA OF STEWY STINKER. A wild cowboy story with zany cartoon pictures—a real hit.

Butterworth, Nick. A YEAR IN PERCY'S PARK. A collection of four stories, two of them with big fold-out maps at the end, that take us through the adventures of the four seasons with Percy the park keeper and the animals in his park.

Ardizzone, Edward. TIM AND GINGER (and many other Tim books). Tim and his friends survive fabulous adventures and mishaps, run-ins with cruel adults, and fights in the school yard (always returning home to warm beds, loving parents, and hot chocolate). Tim manages to be noble and wise (as well as almost always right) without being too nauseating.

Bayley, Nicola. THE MOUSEHOLE CAT. A great story about a great storm that comes up in Mousehole Cove, caused by the great and terrible Mousehole Cat—with a greatly-good and heart-warming ending.

Profound Truths

These books pass on the lessons of life we all learn (and relearn) about the importance of love, marriage, endurance, art, play, perseverance, and contentment.

Lionni, Leo. FREDERICK. A little mouse stores up treasures for winter that prove more lasting than seeds and nuts.

Piper, Watty. THE LITTLE ENGINE THAT COULD. Illustrated by George and Doris Hauman. A story of perseverance—remembering the puffing refrain of the little train, "I think I can, I think I can," is what has pulled many of us through to the end of difficult projects.

Hoban, Russell. THE LITTLE BRUTE FAMILY. The story of the unattractive Brute family whose members snarl, howl, push, pinch, and scold their way through life until Baby Brute finds a "little wandering lost good feeling" and brings it home. The family is soon so transformed (but for appearance) that they change their name to "Nice." We know the book sounds didactic, but it is delightful.

Buckley, Helen. MOONLIGHT KITE. Illustrated by Elsie Primavera. A luminescent book about three monks who relive their childhood through a kite left by some children near their (supposedly deserted) monastery.

Schwartz, Ellen. MR. BELINSKY'S BAGELS. Illustrated by Stefan Czernecki. Mr. Belinsky makes bagels, especially for his three favourite customers, until "Bon Bon Bakery" goes into business across the street. Mr. Belinsky responds to the competition by baking "oatmeal cookies and blackberry tarts, pecan pies and apple strudel," neglecting bagels and his three loyal customers until he remembers his true calling: "I make bagels. Bagels is what I make. And that's that."

Levitin, Sonia. THE MAN WHO KEPT HIS HEART IN A BUCKET. Illustrated by Jerry Pinkney. A young man discovers that the only sure way to keep his heart is to give it away.

Wilde, Oscar. THE SELFISH GIANT. A giant keeps children out of his walled garden—till he learns the meaning of love. Two excellent illustrators of this "Easter" story are Michael Foreman and Lisbeth Zwerger. THE HAPPY PRINCE. Jane Ray's illustrations are a superb match for this story of earthly glory given up in compassionate love and the far greater glory given in return by God.

Bartone, Elisa. PEPPE THE LAMPLIGHTER. Illustrated by Ted Lewin (illustrator of THE ALWAYS PRAYER SHAWL). As Peppe discovers, even the very lowly job of lamplighter, faithfully and earnestly done, brings light not only to Little Italy (in New York City) but also to his family and to life itself. Each lamp he lights becomes for him "a small flame of promise for tomorrow." A beautiful story for us all to remember in *whatever* job we have, however lowly and mundane.

Hermes, Patricia. WHEN SNOW LAY SOFT ON THE MOUNTAIN. Illustrated by Leslie Baker with luminous, almost Japanese-style water colours. The story of Hallie who walks with her father on Hairy Bear Mountain as he shows her the secrets of the seasons and she tells him her simple wishes: oranges at Christmas and a certain unattainable doll . . . .

Paterson, Katherine (reteller). THE TALE OF THE MANDARIN DUCKS. Illustrated by Leo and Diane Dillon. A retelling of a Japanese tale by a favourite writer. *Really*—a book about fidelity in marriage. Another excellent retelling (by Sumiko Yagawa—and translated by Katherine Paterson) of a Japanese classic: THE CRANE WIFE. Illustrated by Suekichi Akaba.

Books about Books

Book lovers will recognize themselves in these!

Winch, John. THE OLD WOMAN WHO LOVED TO READ. An old woman leaves the city and moves to the Australian "outback" to find a quiet and peaceful place to read. All year she is plagued by rurality—unexpected animal guests, fruit to be harvested, summer fires, fall floods—until *finally* she has time to read (only to fall asleep over her book).

Stewart, Sarah. THE LIBRARY. Illustrated by her husband, David Small. Every true *reader* will find a soulmate in Elizabeth Brown and empathize with her dilemma—what to do with all her books. A deeply satisfying book for any lover of books.

Polacco, Patricia. THE BEE TREE. This is *definitely* a story with a Lesson: a girl doesn't feel like reading, so her grandfather takes her on a hunt for a bee tree (everyone else in the area joins in). When the hunt is over, her grandfather explains the similarity between hunting for a bee tree and finding sweetness (adventure, knowledge, wisdom) in a book. See also THANK YOU, MR. FALKER about a girl with a learning disorder whose fifth grade teacher teaches her to read.

Issues

Adults often try to foist ISSUES such as divorce, death, AIDS, etc., on children in the guise of books. Rarely does a book with such a 'message' succeed. However, here are a few books which deal with ISSUES without being sickeningly didactic and moralistic.

Aging

Zolotow, Charlotte. I KNOW A LADY. Pictures by James Stevenson. A comfortable and satisfying story about the lady next door who knows the children in the neighbourhood by name and who gives then flowers and treats according to the seasons.

Burton, Virginia Lee. THE LITTLE HOUSE. MIKE MULLIGAN AND HIS STEAM SHOVEL. KATY AND THE BIG SNOW. Three classics that plant strong values to counteract our throw-away culture.

Fox, Mem. WILFRID GORDON MCDONALD PARTRIDGE. Illustrated by Julie Vivas. A fine book in which a child living next to a nursing home learns about the loss—and meaning—of memory.

Rylant, Cynthia. THE OLD WOMAN WHO NAMED THINGS. Illustrated by Kathryn Brown. An old woman is so lonely, having outlived all her friends, that she gives names to her bed, her car, her house. But she won't give a name to the lonely puppy that keeps coming by to visit until he stops coming and she gets lonely for him.

Greene, Graham. (The novelist!) THE LITTLE FIRE ENGINE. THE LITTLE TRAIN. Two books about old, neglected and lonely machines (and their old drivers) that win back their place through courageous caring. Illustrated by Edward Ardizzone.

Griffith, Helen V. GEORGIA MUSIC. Pictures by James Stevenson. A girl spends the summer with her grandfather in Georgia. They garden, listen to birds and play the harmonica. But the next summer he is ill and must return with them to Baltimore, where she tries to share with him memories of the Georgia summer they shared.

Miles, Miska. ANNIE AND THE OLD ONE. Illustrated by Peter Parnall in his sparse, desert style. A young Indian girl learns much from her grandmother, including the acceptance of death.

Racism

Polacco, Patricia. CHICKEN SUNDAY. In the spirit of Vera Williams'
   book A CHAIR FOR MY MOTHER, three children earn money
   to buy an Easter bonnet for Miss Eula to wear at the Baptist church
   where she sings in the choir with a voice like "slow thunder and
   sweet rain." After church they enjoyed Chicken Sunday: "fried
   chicken, collard greens, hoppin' john." An inobtrusively interracial
   story.

Foreignness

Aliki. MARIANTHE'S STORY: PAINTED WORDS AND SPOKEN
   MEMORIES is the autobiography of Aliki. In PAINTED WORDS,
   Marianthe begins school in a new country. Unable to speak the language, she draws pictures of her life and the country she left. Turn
   the book over and in SPOKEN MEMORIES Marianthe, using all
   her pictures as illustrations, tells the story of her past in the language
   she has just learned.

Piping down the valleys wild,
Piping songs of pleasant glee,
On a cloud I saw a child,
And he laughing said to me:

"Pipe a song about a Lamb!"
So I piped with merry cheer.
"Piper, pipe that song again";
So I piped; he wept to hear.

"Drop thy pipe, thy happy pipe;
Sing thy songs of happy cheer!"
So I sang the same again,
While he wept with joy to hear.

"Piper, sit thee down and write
In a book, that all may read."
So he vanished from my sight;
And I plucked a hollow reed,

And I made a rural pen,
And I stained the water clear,
And I wrote my happy songs
Every child may joy to hear.

—William Blake
"Introduction to Songs of Innocence"

4

Music

Perhaps it seems like music should not be included in a reading list, but melodies and words are so tied together that it does not seem a good idea to separate them. Think of all the Christmas carols that are so memorable they will still be sung in July. And remember all the chanted nursery rhymes, bedtime lullabies, and action songs made into children's books.

Music can be thought of as a different setting for words than illustrations. Just as a book in which the illustrations and text complement each other is better than a book in which words and pictures seem disconnected or disjointed, so also a musical setting and text must match. A book which combines words, music, and pictures *well* is truly a work of art.

Singing can be a good way to set the mood for a bedtime story session or to gather the attention of a distracted listener. (Lest you believe this is just useful for children, think of how music is used on adults: to announce a particular news program, to begin a sporting event, to conclude a religious service, etc.) Singing together is a way to share an experience *and* a book; everyone can participate, especially when sitting still and keeping quiet seems impossible.

Finally, singing a book seems to place it even deeper into a child's memory than reading it. Music may be a more direct way to reach the soul. Or, as Shakespeare put it, music is "the food of love"!

Collections

Fox, Dan, ed. GO IN AND OUT THE WINDOW. An illustrated songbook for young people; commentary by Claude Marks. Produced by the Metropolitan Museum of Art (New York)—and wonderfully illustrated from their huge collection, this is a beautiful book with most of the best children's songs in easy-to-sing (and play) arrangements. (Non-Americans might need a supplement to balance the American patriotic songs!)

LULLABIES: AN ILLUSTRATED SONGBOOK. Music arranged by Richard Kapp. Another production from the Metropolitan Museum of Art which follows the same format as GO IN AND OUT THE WINDOW (in fact, it even repeats a few pictures) and is of the same high quality. These two are always on the piano.

THE LAP-TIME SONG AND PLAY BOOK. Edited by Jane Yolen. Illustrated by Margot Tomes. ROUND AND ROUND THE GARDEN. Selected by Sarah Williams. Illustrated by Ian Beck. Here are the early playsongs with words and music for those who didn't grow up knowing these as a bedrock of childhood fun. Such playsongs are good for distracting a child while changing her diaper, while waiting for a bus, and other desperate moments that need an injection of joy.

Headington, Christopher. SWEET SLEEP. A collection of lullabies, poems and cradle songs. A sensationally soporific selection!

THE LAURA INGALLS WILDER SONGBOOK. Edited by Eugenia Garson. Contains all the songs mentioned in the LITTLE HOUSE books, and has illustrations from the books as well.

SONG OF ROBIN HOOD. Selected and edited by Anne Malcolmson. Music arranged by Grace Castagnetta. Illustrated by Virginia Lee Burton. If you are a fan of Robin Hood, English Ballads, or Virginia Lee Burton, this is a necessary book. The songs are long, the tunes traditional, and the drawings are tiny. All of this might be a deterrent if everything weren't so carefully and beautifully done. There is a glossary at the back to help with the more archaic words. The tunes are beautiful and as historically accurate as possible. The illustrations are incredibly detailed: every song has specific flora as part of the design and *all* the verses (except those within the musical notation) are individually illustrated.

❦

Individual Songs

Harrison, Ted (Illustrator). O CANADA. Vibrant illustrations for each province and territory accompany the song. After absorbing this book, you might actually hear your child belting out the song at Canadian sporting events instead of mumbling along with the rest of the crowd.

Kovalski, Maryann (Illustrator). THE WHEELS ON THE BUS. Words, pictures and tunes for a traditional song all children love.

Langstreet, John. OVER IN THE MEADOW. Pictures by Feodor Rojankovsky. Gentle sketches of animal families illustrate the song, which involves both counting and animal life.

❦

Christmas Songbooks

MY BOOK OF CHRISTMAS CAROLS. Fourteen of the best, collected by B. Rosenkrans and illustrated by Jane Dyer.

USBORNE BOOK OF CHRISTMAS CAROLS. Simple arrangements, but all the verses are included! Illustrated by Stephen Cartwright.

JOY TO THE WORLD! Carols selected by Maureen Forrester. Arranged by Charles Heller. Illustrated by Frances Tyrrell. Twelve Christmas carols (some old, some new).

✣

Individual Christmas Carols

THE FRIENDLY BEASTS: A TRADITIONAL CHRISTMAS CAROL. Illustrated by Sarah Chamberlain. This hymn in which all the animals of the stable bring gifts to the Christ Child is well loved and visually rich in detail. Chamberlain's warm and loving pictures reinforce the verse-by-verse perspective of each animal. Both the hymn and her artwork keep the child as the audience focus—a rare thing in any modern children's book.

THE HURON CAROL. By Father Jean de Brebeuf. Illustrated by Frances Tyrrell. Over 350 years ago, Father Brebeuf, one of the earliest and best of the early missionaries to the native people of North America, composed this carol of the coming of Jesus into the life of the world of the Huron Indians near Fort Ste Marie in Ontario. Tyrrell's illustrations contextualize into that snowy northern setting the longing and joy which all of us who hear this story share. In word and art, the book is an example of the way the response of every tribe and nation to Jesus (see Revelation 21:26) can bring new light to our understanding of Biblical story. Contains a brief history and the music of the carol.

WOODLAND CHRISTMAS. Illustrated by Frances Tyrrell. Tyrrell has kept the original words to the Twelve Days of Christmas while using the illustrations to show the courtship and marriage of two elaborately dressed bears. Northern animals make up the twelve gifts (the four calling birds are loons, etc.).

Granfield, Linda. SILENT NIGHT: THE SONG FROM HEAVEN. Art by Nellie and Ernest Hofer. In the same year, two superb books arrived to tell us the history of this favourite Christmas carol. Both this book and the next tell not only how the hymn came to be written, but also of soldiers singing the song across battle lines on Christmas Eve during World War I.

Hodges, Margaret. SILENT NIGHT: THE SONG AND ITS STORY. Illustrated by Tim Ladwig. See previous entry.

SILENT NIGHT. Illustrated by Susan Jeffers. An evocative evening setting for the hymnal telling of the events of that long ago silent and splendorous night.

GOOD KING WENCESLAS. By John Mason Neale. Illustrated by Christopher Manson. Medieval style woodcuts in a treasure of a book.

❧

Hymns for the Rest of the Church Year

Hymns can be a way of introducing theology, poetry, and music. Singing them at bedtime or mealtime is a wonderful way of sharing this literary heritage with our children. (In church, they may sing mainly choruses, which often have a distinct lack of literary beauty and should not be the only Christian musical inheritance we leave for the next generation.)

BE THOU MY VISION. Words translated by Eleanor Hull from ancient Irish. Tradition Irish melody. Like many other favourite hymns, this one has a folk melody, a 'hummable' tune honed by generations.

FAIREST LORD JESUS. Words by "Gesangbuch" Munster. Silesian folk melody. A hymn with vivid creation images.

LIKE A RIVER GLORIOUS. Words by Frances Havergal. Music by James Mountain. Flowing words and melody with a chorus referring to perfect peace and rest. (Perhaps a parental favourite?)

CHILDREN OF THE HEAVENLY FATHER. Words by Lina Sandell. Swedish Melody. A comforting and soothing hymn about the care our Father gives us, with lovely, specific images, including stars in heaven and birds in nests.

TAKE MY LIFE AND LET IT BE. Words by Frances Havergal. Music by Mozart. This is a wonderful hymn to mime or make up a dance to. It is full of specific bodily ways we can give ourselves to God.

I FEEL THE WINDS OF GOD. Words by Jesse Adams. Tradition English and Irish melody (Kingsfold). We are a ship and God is the wind blowing behind us our entire lives.

MAY THE MIND OF CHRIST MY SAVIOUR. Words by Kate B. Wilkinson. Music by C. Barham-Gould. Filled with lasting images of how to live out our Christian life.

MORNING HAS BROKEN. Words by Eleanor Farjeon. Old Gaelic melody. A joyful, light-filled testimony to the restorative powers of our Creator and Sustainer.

HYMNS II. (In the spiral edition.) Published by InterVarsity Press. Seems to have separated most of the wheat from the chaff—and certainly has avoided the worst. Has all but two of the above hymns.

In childhood sing-song is not a defect. It is simply the first form of rhythmical sensibility; crude itself, but a good symptom not a bad one. This metronomic regularity, this sway of the whole body to the metre simply as metre, is the basis which makes possible all later variations and subtleties. For there are no variations except for those who know a norm, and no subtleties for those who have not grasped the obvious.

—C. S. Lewis

A child cannot help but begin life with a love of poetry if you consider that the first sound he hears is a poem: the rhythmic beat of his mother's heart.

—Jim Trelease

A word aptly spoken is like apples of gold in settings of silver.

—Proverbs 25:11

. . . children saturated with poetry are not likely to become cynical in the world of adulthood or to spend their last days in psychopathic wards. Books make the inner world of man, just as clothes make the outer one; and poetry makes the very soul come alive.

—Calvin Ryan

Poetry is a way of taking life by the throat.

—Robert Frost

5

Poetry

It was not on a whim of wordplay that St. John claimed, "In the beginning was the Word, and the Word was with God, and the Word was God" (John 1:1). The Word spoke all things into being, into *beginning*, and the Word, in scripture and in Jesus, is the beginning of knowledge—knowledge of the inner consistency and cohesiveness that make all things, all creation, knowable.

The Word, made flesh and blood in Jesus, is also the beginning of communication, the beginning of speech, the source of that inner logic—*logos*—that holds words from flying apart into an incomprehensible cacophony. Through the Word at the heart of creation, we can communicate with God and with each other.

The Word as God is therefore at the *beginning* of all being, all knowledge, and all communication. And words are maybe the richest "gene" in the genesis of our spiritual "genetic code" for being made in the image and likeness of God.

We use words—and yet we are not the Word. Inside of us there is so *much more* than we can say with words. God can say in response to his creation through Word, "That's good"; we are always slightly frustrated by the discrepancies between our words and our feelings. And yet, though we do not have Word—that speaking forth and holding together of all knowledge and communication, all being and feeling, we do have words. We have the building-blocks—words—of that perfect creation by the Word.

Poetry, more than any other form of literature, teaches us how to play with these blocks. We learn, through the succinct care of poetic phrasing, not only the particularity of meaning in words; but also the nuances of history and context, the music of sibilants and gutturals, rhythm and rhyme, and the resonance of metaphor, image and symbol. Poetry comes closest to the exactitude of the Word. Its word choices and patterns teach us and our children how to express joy and delight, pain and sorrow—how to tell in words the volumes hidden in our souls.

In his book on the Psalms, Eugene Peterson captures the wonder of both poetry and the Psalms:

> *Poetry* is language used with personal intensity . . . . Poets use words to drag us into the depth of reality itself. They do it not by reporting on how life is, but by pushing—pulling us into the middle of it. Poetry grabs for the jugular.

When we read poems to our children, we begin to unwrap the great, strong gift of Word.

✿

Nursery Rhymes

Mother Goose is wonderful for literary development but, since the prime age is 0-5 years, when reading to very young children try to avoid editions that have only one illustration for every 3-4 rhymes. Telling from memory during play and work is the best use for them. This list is roughly ordered from "youngest" to "oldest."

THE REAL MOTHER GOOSE. HUSKY BLUE, RED, GREEN. For the *first* Mother Goose (Not counting lapsongs and fingerplays), use these boardbook volumes—small, easy to hold, and one picture/ rhyme per page.

THE LAP-TIME SONG AND PLAY BOOK. Edited with a helpful introduction by Jane Yolen, Illustrated by Margot Tomes. Musical arrangements (with chords!) by Adam Stemple. A good beginner how-to for those who want to use finger-plays and lap games, but don't know how.

ROUND AND ROUND THE GARDEN. Compiled by Sarah Williams. Illustrated by Ian Beck. An excellent collection of play rhymes for children that has more rhymes than Yolen's book but no tunes.

MOTHER GOOSE. Illustrated by Tomie de Paola. Excellent for very young children.

THE TALL BOOK OF MOTHER GOOSE. Illustrated by Feodor Rojankovsky. A wide selection of rhymes, each with a good illustration, in a fun, tall book—one of our favourites.

MY VERY FIRST MOTHER GOOSE. Edited by Iona Opie. Illustrated by Rosemary Wells. This is a lovely book because of its structure— divided into 4 chapters; its characters—a cast of quirky animals; and the subtle humor in the drawings which keep the adult reader's attention once the words are memorized.

HERE COMES MOTHER GOOSE. A good collection for very young children by the same wonderful team, although the other is slightly superior. They do take license with the old rhyme about what little girls and boys are made of!

SYLVIA LONG'S MOTHER GOOSE. Collection of all the old favourites, many of which are left out in recent politically-correct versions. One rhyme per illustration—all the characters are dressed up animals.

APPLEY DAPPLEY'S NURSERY RHYME BOOK. CECILY PARSLEY'S NURSERY RHYMES. Collected and illustrated by Beatrix Potter in her little books for little people.

THE ORIGINAL MOTHER GOOSE. Illustrated by Blanche Fisher Wright. Originally published in 1916. More rhymes than you'll ever read (not all are illustrated). The pictures are old-fashioned yet clear. This is a classic.

❋

Multi-Poet Collections

These books are filled with carefully-chosen, well-loved and time-tested poems. Get one or two good anthologies that you and your children can live with and love, and use the library for enrichment.

ANIMAL CRACKERS. Collected and illustrated by Jane Dyer. A wonderful compilation of poems about Food, Animals, Playtime, Seasons, and other important aspects of life. Many of the poems and rhymes are familiar, but there are just enough new ones to spice up the bunch. And each one has an illustration!

TALKING LIKE THE RAIN. Selected by X. J. Kennedy and Dorothy Kennedy. Illustrated by Jane Dyer. A superbly-done collection to choose as a family poetry book.

A SMALL CHILD'S BOOK OF VERSE. Edited by Pelagie Doane. A beautifully-illustrated, well-chosen collection.

NOISY RHYMES. GIGGLY RHYMES. Collected by Jill Bennett. Illustrated by Nick Sharratt. Little collections of fun-to-read poems that might help win over a child—or a parent—who finds poetry hard to like.

THE RANDOM HOUSE BOOK OF POETRY FOR CHILDREN. Selected and introduced by Jack Prelutsky. Illustrations by Arnold Lobel. This is a thorough collection of 572 poems complete with old and new authors. It includes a fair amount of delightfully disrespectful and simply silly poems. A childhood hit!

PUFFINS: This paperback publisher has put out a number of good collections such as POEMS FOR SEVEN-YEAR-OLDS AND UNDER; THE YOUNG PUFFIN BOOK OF VERSE.

A CHILDREN'S BOOK OF VERSE. Edited by Marjorie Rogers. Illustrated by Eric Kincaid. An unusual collection including many old story poems. Published in England by Brimax.

Resource Collections

These are all tomes which are very helpful as resources but lack the appealing illustrations crucial for getting children into poetry.

THIS LITTLE PUFFIN . . . . Compiled by Elizabeth Matterson. Melody and words for nursery games, rhymes, and songs. Not enough illustrations to use with very young children, but a great resource.

THE OXFORD NURSERY RHYME BOOK. Edited by Iona and Peter Opie. A fine, organized collection—starts off with all the early baby play poems and ends with lyrics and tales. Good, though small, illustrations for most of the rhymes. See also their THE OXFORD DICTIONARY OF NURSERY RHYMES. A *complete* collection with detailed notes on the history and wording of each rhyme. Both of these books are superb resource books; the DICTIONARY is invaluable in giving parents opportunity to turn repetition into research.

ALL THE SILVER PENNIES. Edited by Blanche Jennings Thompson. An introduction for each poem, and pictures for most—a good collection of old favourites.

COME HITHER. Edited by Walter de la Mare. A wonderful collection of his anthologies. Few pictures, but the last third "About and Roundabout," which includes helpful comments on the poems, is an education in poetry appreciation.

FAVORITE POEMS OLD AND NEW. Edited by Helen Ferris. A real tome to lug around, with very few pictures, but an excellent collection to have available when hunting for poems on a particular subject.

✿

Single Poet Collections

Eliot, T. S. OLD POSSUM'S BOOK OF PRACTICAL CATS. By one of the best modern English poets. (Text for the long-running musical, CATS). Several editions by different illustrators. Try the simplest and oldest one, illustrated by Nicholas Bentley.

Farjeon, Eleanor. THE CHILDREN'S BELLS. Includes her famous poem and hymn, "Morning Has Broken." One of her many books of poems.

Frost, Robert. A SWINGER OF BIRCHES: POEMS OF ROBERT FROST FOR YOUNG PEOPLE. Illustrated by Peter Koep and introduced by Clifton Fadiman. A beautifully introduction to this fine poet whose richly drawn descriptions open the door to an awareness of imagery.

Frost, Robert. POETRY FOR YOUNG PEOPLE: ROBERT FROST. Edited by Gary Schmidt. Illustrated by Henri Sorensen. Schmidt starts the book with a short biography of Frost. The book is organized by the seasons and includes brief notes by Schmidt to enhance the reader's appreciation and understanding of the poems.

de Gasztold, Carmen Bernos. PRAYERS FROM THE ARK. Translated by Rumer Godden. Be sure to get the edition finely illustrated by

Barry Moser. With humour and compassion, these poem/prayers capture the longing of the animals *and* of many of us.

Hughes, Shirley. RHYMES FOR ANNIE ROSE. OUT AND ABOUT. Poems which are simple for children to understand and remember. Don't be surprised to hear this poetry repeated back to you, as in, "I *do* like mud!" (shouted while stomping in puddles).

Lear, Edward (author *and* illustrator). THE COMPLETE NONSENSE BOOK. Classic jingles and limericks. Children will be mesmerized by the rhyme—and adults by the pictures.

Milne, A. A. WHEN WE WERE VERY YOUNG. NOW WE ARE SIX. Illustrated by Ernest Shepard. Buy the little books by the author of the Pooh stories (i.e., not the big collections).

O'Neill, Mary. HAILSTONES AND HALIBUT BONES. Thoughtful, descriptive poems about twelve colours. A favourite poetry book. Reissued recently in an edition illustrated by John Wallner. Or, look for the older illustrations by Leonard Weisgard.

Stevenson, Robert Louis. A CHILD'S GARDEN OF VERSES. A classic available in many editions by different illustrators. A distinguished edition bringing together a number of illustrators has been put together by Cooper Edens and published by Chronicle Books.

Individual Poems

Field, Rachel. GENERAL STORE. Pictures by Nancy Winslow Parker. Captures the wonder of the myriad of things one could buy at the old "general store" (or the old dime store that has faded out in the brilliant glitz of the _____ Marts).

Frost, Robert. STOPPING BY WOODS ON A SNOWY EVENING. Beautiful pictures by Susan Jeffers balance Frost's words.

Lear, Edward. THE JUMBLIES. Illustrated by Ted Rand. Simple yet fantastical pictures illustrate this strange poem. THE OWL AND THE PUSSYCAT. Illustrated by Jan Brett. Lear's playfulness with words and Brett's ability to tell a layered story with pictures combine to make a wonderful book.

Noyes, Alfred. THE HIGHWAYMAN. Fine line drawings by Charles Keeping for this old read-aloud favourite.

Poe, Edgar. ANNABEL LEE. Illustrated by Gilles Tibo. Hauntingly beautiful illustrations for a hauntingly musical poem.

Service, Robert. THE CREMATION OF SAM McGEE. THE SHOOTING OF DAN McGREW. Both vibrantly illustrated by the Canadian artist, Ted Harrison. These are verse stories with a driving urgency of rhythm and rhyme that match the wild wonder of the strange tales of the Canadian North. Gripping to read aloud.

Tolkien, J. R. R. BILBO'S LAST SONG. Illustrated by Pauline Baynes (also illustrator of the Narnia books). A beautiful introduction to THE HOBBIT and THE LORD OF THE RINGS.

If we don't know the Bible and the central stories of Greek and Roman literature, we can still read books and see plays, but our knowledge of literature can't grow, just as our knowledge of mathematics can't grow if we don't learn the multiplication table.

—Northrop Frye

Not Herod, not Caiaphas, not Pilate, not Judas, ever contrived to fasten upon Jesus Christ the reproach of insipidity; that final indignity was left for pious hands to inflict. To make of His story something that could neither startle, nor shock, nor terrify, nor excite, nor inspire a living soul is to crucify the Son of God afresh and put Him to an open shame. . . . Let me tell you, good Christian people, an honest writer would be ashamed to treat a nursery tale as you have treated the greatest drama in history. . . .

—Dorothy L. Sayers

The disciples came up and asked, "Why do you tell stories?" He replied, "You've been given insight into God's kingdom. You know how it works. Not everyone has this gift, this insight; it hasn't been given to them. Whenever someone has a ready heart for this, the insights and understandings flow freely. But if there is no readiness, any trace of receptivity soon disappears. That's why I tell stories: to create readiness, to nudge the people toward receptive insight. In their present state they can stare till doomsday and not see it, listen till they're blue in the face and not get it."

—Matthew 13: 10-13

6

Bible Stories

The richest literary heritage we can offer our children is the wealth of story in the Bible. It is—for heart and mind, body and soul—a heritage of practical wisdom, of psychological understanding, and of rich wording honed by centuries of oral retellings. Most importantly, it is the story which God is telling: God's Word, embodied in human words.

These stories don't flinch from the jealousies, fears, and downright meanness that characterized human beings a long time ago and which we continue to recognize in ourselves. This book of books tells both the painful story of human struggle and the grand story of God's willingness to share in both the struggle and the pain. The stories don't founder in either the morass of human bitterness or the sternness of God's judgment. They tell the whole truth: that God is not only a God of justice, but also of mercy; that God hates every sort of evil, but loves every single one of his children; that God is infinitely beyond all we can understand, but involved in the most infinitessimal concerns of our lives.

As the pattern of the Great Story unfolds in story after story, we keep discovering the truth about the Biblical heroes, and about ourselves: that, in the words of Isaiah, "We all, like sheep, have gone astray, each of us has turned to our own way . . ." (Isaiah 53:6). We all sin. But that is not the end of the story. After that bad news comes the Good News that God is also Jesus, the Good Shepherd, come to stand with us and for us. That is the true, longed-for "happy ending" to which (as J. R. R. Tolkien affirms) all the great fairy tales point.

Why then, when we try to convey this heritage to our children, do we often use cheap little books with tawdry illustrations which in efforts to "nicen up" the often brutal, earthy realities of the Biblical originals, lose much of the blood-red richness of their complex, whole truth? Worse yet, why do we often settle for pedantic, moralizing stories which teach us not to lie or cheat or steal, but lose the wonder and joy of God's story? We often cringe at both the nastiness of human sin and the firmness of God's justice, and at the same time find it difficult to accept the inexhaustible depth and breadth of God's love and mercy.

When we are tempted to button up our theology in the storm-proof cloak of the average Sunday School story, we need to ask ourselves if these stories tell the Truth: the whole story, both the sad and the glad, the disturbing justice and the comforting mercy, the agony and the ecstasy. Our children need to see the balance of sin with grace, of justice with love, of judgment with mercy. In reading Bible stories to them, we teach them the balance which permeates God's great Story—and can permeate their story.

(For more help in regaining a sense of perspective on this greatest of Stories—read Tolkien's essay "On Fairy Stories," Northrop Frye's THE GREAT CODE, and the plays—and introductions—in Dorothy L. Sayer's great collection, THE MAN BORN TO BE KING.)

Picture Books of Bible Stories

As in **Picture Books**, *these books are roughly ordered from "youngest" to "oldest."*

Butterworth, Nick and Mick Inkpen. STORIES JESUS TOLD. Very well-written and well-illustrated little stories retelling some of the parables of Jesus.

PSALM 23. Illustrated by Tim Ladwig. A city setting gives new depth to this favourite psalm.

TO EVERY THING THERE IS A SEASON. Illustrated by Leo and Diane Dillon. All 15 phrases in this excerpt from Ecclesiastes are illustrated in different styles, including an Egyptian tomb mural, a European woodcut, a Greek classic vase painting, a Russian icon, and an example of stone-cut Inuit art.

Jonas, Ann. AARDVARKS, DISEMBARK! Biblically accurate in telling the story, but when it gets down to describing the animals on the ark, it goes far beyond the usual elephants and kangaroos to a full, alphabetic menagerie from the global diversity of the animal kingdom. Complete with an appendix giving details of pronunciation, description and location for each of these often-unheard-of, but definitely real travellers on Noah's Ark.

Johnson, James Weldon. THE CREATION. Illustrated by James E. Ransome. A great, grand, glorious telling of the Genesis story in true Southern Gospel sermonic form.

THE STORY OF THE CREATION. Illustrated by Jane Ray. A beautiful, richly coloured celebration of the day-by-day choreography of creation. Ray's illustrations help us see the wholeness of pattern in the Genesis story. NOAH'S ARK. Richly beautiful without being overdone.

Spier, Peter. NOAH'S ARK. JONAH. Wordless and wonderful. These books capture the gritty realities of the messiness of Noah's wild menagerie and the sloshy sea life of being caught in a whale.

Pilling, Ann (compiler) BEFORE I GO TO SLEEP. Illustrated by Kady MacDonald Denton. A gleaning of the best from poetry, prayers, Bible stories—all for the bedtime joy of reading. May be most valuable as a resource for parents.

❧
Faith-Filled Stories

Lindbergh, Reeve. THE CIRCLE OF DAYS. Illustrated by Cathie Felstead. Reeve Lindbergh adapts the "Canticle of the Sun," Saint Francis of Assisi's hymn of praise for *all* aspects of life. It is simple, beautiful, and direct: "For brother sleep, and sister death, who tend the borders of our breath." The collage paintings are a perfect enrichment of the text. An excellent introduction to prayer and reasons to praise God.

Hunt, Angela Elwell (reteller). THE TALE OF THREE TREES. Illustrated by Tim Jonke. Three trees play important parts in the life of Jesus. Good for Easter as well as Christmas.

Wilde, Oscar. THE SELFISH GIANT. Not a Bible story, but a modern fairy tale integrated with Christian meaning. Be sure to get an unabriged, unedited version: some versions edit the Christian imagery out!

❧
Books Based on the Bible

Lindvall, Ella K. READ-ALOUD BIBLE STORIES. Four volumes. Illustrated by Ken Renczenski. Expensive—but worth the money: these books are geared to a very young audience in both pictures and prose—and young children respond! Volume 3 is a good starter; it begins with creation and ends with the birth of Jesus. Also available in small, individual story books.

Sattgast, L. J. THE RHYME BIBLE. Illustrated by Toni Goffe. Rhyming stories from both the Old and New Testaments with entertaining (but a little cutsie) illustrations. The rhythm of the story is bouncy enough for babies, while the text is interesting enough for early readers.

de Paola, Tomie. TOMIE DE PAOLA'S BOOK OF BIBLE STORIES. Excellent for young children. New International Version text. He also has done two very good Picture Bible Story books: THE PARABLES OF JESUS and THE MIRACLES OF JESUS.

BIBLE STORIES FOR CHILDREN. Retold by Geoffrey Horn and Arthur Cavenaugh. Illustrated by Arvis Stewart. A beautifully-crafted Bible story book—both text and illustrations capture the greatness of the Biblical narrative. Far and away our favourite of all the Bible story books for children.

Delval, Marie-Helene. THE READER'S DIGEST BIBLE FOR CHILDREN. Illustrated by Ulises Wensell. Beautiful illustrations accompany simplified Old and New Testament stories. Don't be turned off by the "Reader's Digest" in the title: this is a very high-quality book.

THE KINGFISHER CHILDREN'S BIBLE. Ann Pilling, reteller; Kady MacDonald Denton, illustrator—the same team that did BEFORE I GO TO SLEEP. Unusual in its inclusion of selections from "Song of Songs" and the Minor Prophets.

Graham, Ruth. ONE WINTRY NIGHT. Illustrated by Richard Jesse Watson. A young boy takes shelter in a woman's mountain cabin. While they are snowbound, the woman tells the boy the Christmas story, starting with Creation and ending with the Resurrection. Watson put four years of thought and expertise into the splendidly-detailed pictures. They are stunning!

THE PICTURE BIBLE. Yes—comics. But children love it and read it.

McKissack, Patricia and Fredrick. LET MY PEOPLE GO. Pictures by James E. Ransome. The McKissacks have interspersed twelve Old Testament stories with stories about the lives of fictional characters: Charlotte Jefferies and her father Price, a former slave turned blacksmith. As the McKissacks point out about the Bible, "The ideas that these ancient stories hold are not for one people, at one time, in one place. They are for all of us, for all times, everywhere."

Schmidt, Gary D. THE BLESSING OF THE LORD—STORIES FROM
THE OLD AND NEW TESTAMENTS. Illustrated by Dennis Nolan.
With integrity, Schmidt has added depth and personality to famil-
iar Bible stories.

✤

Christmas Stories

The Incarnation—God becoming a child—is the child's best connection point to the simultaneity of supernatural and natural that is at
the heart of the Christian understanding of all being—and at the heart of
faith. When we look at the birth of Jesus, the whole story seems designed
for a child; it is not only a story of a child, it is also a story which includes
all those parts of creation that fascinate a child—sheep, angels, barns,
mommy and daddy, stars, visitors, presents—not to mention the don-
keys, cows, camels, doves and spiders that seem to have snuck into various tellings. And who knows, maybe in such child-responsive imaginings,
these tellings have edged closer and closer to God's own inclusiveness of
the whole of his creation in his Good News.

We would do well by our children if we followed God's storytelling
pattern—the lean of his story toward the ear of a child. If we think that
God didn't have an ear toward a potential child audience then we fail to
take children (and God's regard for them) seriously. We can also rob the
incarnation of most of its power by underestimating what *all* it means
about God and his relationship to us, and to our children, that he was
born of Mary—a human baby born to a human mother. And we give
little honour to God as the Storyteller who is in himself the source of all
that makes stories good: imagery and detail, plots with innuendo and
multi-leveled meaning, audience awareness and so forth and so on, world
of story without end. In telling the Christmas Story to our children, we
bring God's Story and their story together—and THAT IS GOOD
NEWS.

Those of us in the Northern hemisphere can make good use of a rich
detail that underlies the whole story of the Good News: the coming of
light into darkness. In those darkening late afternoons or in the full dark
of the bedtime hour, we can light candles, perhaps on an advent wreath,

and let the light of The Story glow with the candles through the surrounding darkness. God's light may burn more brightly in both our hearts and the hearts and imaginations of our children if we recreate the dark setting, such as was the shepherds' nightly vigil or the far-off wise men's night sky watch. For, long ago, God's lights of angel choir and bright star burned though darkness, calling to shepherds, to wise men—and to our children: "Come and see Jesus."

Not all of these books are God's Story of the birth of His Son, but they are on this list because each one provides a glimmer of the light that shines into every darkness. In a time when we sometimes fear that the Light of the World is being systematically extinguished, the very wealth—in number and goodness—of the books on this list is almost an embarrassment of riches and certainly a brilliant beacon to truth.

❧

Christmas Picture Books

Again, as in all the picture book sections, these are roughly ordered from "youngest" to "oldest."

Slate, Joseph. WHO'S COMING TO OUR HOUSE? Illustrated by Ashley Wolff. The simple and childlike refrain of this title builds a growing wonder and joy as the animals of the stable first sense that something's happening and then watch Mary and Joseph wend their way to the stable. A perfect book for very young children; they'll join the refrain in more ways than one!

Rossetti, Christina. WHAT CAN I GIVE HIM? Illustrated by Debi Gliori. Several stories interplay in a superbly-illustrated book that, reminiscent of Tolstoy's SHOEMAKER MARTIN, reminds us that a gift we can give to the Christ child is our care and love for others. The words are from the fine old Christmas hymn by Christina Rosetti, "In the Bleak Midwinter." "What can I give him, poor as I am? Give him my heart."

Petersham, Maud and Miska. THE CHRIST CHILD. An old and beautiful classic. Richly heraldic pictures balance the richness of the King James wording.

Carlstrom, Nancy White. THE SNOW SPEAKS. Illustrated by Jane Dyer. Descriptions of the wonder of a winter snowfall, replete with snowdrifts and snowplows, culminate in a jubilant finale as snow angels speak the good news of Christmas to Creation—"Glory. Glory. Glory" At heart, this is a book about natural revelation—even the northern snows from the heavens declare the glory of God.

Dunbar, Joyce. THIS IS THE STAR. Illustrated by Gary Blythe (Carnegie Award winner for THE WHALES' SONG). A "This is the House that Jack Built" telling of the birth of Jesus. Though we expect such a format to make the story trite and silly, instead it reiterates our increasing sense of that night's wonder and glory.

Berger, Barbara. THE DONKEY'S DREAM. What is it like to carry Mary and her unborn child? The pictures and words of the dreams of the donkey show us what he cannot tell. These are images used throughout Christian history to convey the meaning of Jesus.

Vivas, Julie. THE NATIVITY. Vivas brings the Incarnation down to earth—as indeed it was!

Kajpust, Melissa. A DOZEN SILK DIAPERS. Illustrated by Veselina Tomova. A fun, warm, sweet, wonderful story of a mother spider and her 40 children who are in the stable when Jesus is born. The spider children are wildly excited about this newcomer and with spider ingenuity figure out ways to get as close as possible. But when the wise men come with their gifts, they worry about what they can give him until their mother hits upon a solution which keeps them all busy—and results in a very useful baby gift.

Akoi, Hisako and Ivan Gantschev. SANTA'S FAVORITE STORY. Brings together (with really excellent balance) Santa, presents, and the good news of the Christ child.

Alavedra, Joan. THEY FOLLOWED A BRIGHT STAR. Illustrated by Ulises Wensell. Though this is first of all the story of the wise men following the star to Jesus, it is also the intriguingly comforting story of five ordinary folk whose dedication to their mundane tasks wouldn't let them follow along. And yet . . . *they* were preparing gifts of water, fish, bread and wine that Jesus used in ways that give gifts to his followers even to this day. This is a simple and good story that gives meaning to ordinary life.

Farber, Norma. WHEN IT SNOWED THAT NIGHT. Illustrated by Petra Mathers. Simple and superb illustrations for simple and superb poems telling of the welcome to Jesus from such diverse figures in creation as hogs, Queens, Mary herself and another mother far away who, in tending her child reminds us that those who "follow the star" of Jesus by means of everyday chores such as mothering give great gifts to the Christ Child.

Collington, Peter. A SMALL MIRACLE. Here in a wordless wonder of a story, is the miracle of the "Magnificat" enacted in the life of a poor old gypsy woman.

Oppel, Kenneth. FOLLOW THAT STAR. Illustrated by Kim LaFave. The announcement by the hosts of heaven probably did stimulate excitement, though maybe not all the hilarious hijinks in this book, as those flocks of sheep were hurried and hustled by night towards Bethlehem. The text is a bit long, but the wildly and exuberantly wondrous story of shepherds and sheep chasing after Jesus is a good and maybe even realistic balance for the plethora of sentimental and sweet retellings.

Watts, Bernadette. THE CHRISTMAS BIRD. A child's humble gift for the Christ Child, a broken wooden bird whistle is transformed into a living singing bird by the touch of the baby King.

Gardam, Catherine. THE ANIMALS' CHRISTMAS. Illustrated by Gavin Rowe. A great tale about how all the animals in a village go missing on Christmas Eve—and are found nearby in the ruins of an old abbey loudly proclaimimg the good news in their own tongue.

The story is a gentle reminder that the whole of creation is telling the glory of God—if we would but listen and hear.

Tolstoy, Leo. THE SHOEMAKER'S DREAM. Retold by Mildred Schell. Illustrated by Masahiro Kasuya. SHOEMAKER MARTIN. Illustrated by Bernadette Watts. Two of several versions of Tolstoy's story of a poor shoemaker who discovered Jesus where he didn't expect to find him.

Van Allsburg, Chris. THE POLAR EXPRESS. A solemn midnight ride to the north pole. Not exactly "sacred"—but it opens a chink in the armor of secular materialism.

Kurelek, William. A NORTHERN NATIVITY. What if . . . Jesus had been born in an igloo, a boxcar, a fishing boat . . . ?

Houston, Gloria. THE YEAR OF THE PERFECT CHRISTMAS TREE. Illustrated by Barbara Cooney. This book brings "recovery," in the Tolkienian sense, to the great gift of a family celebrating Christmas—together.

Menotti, Gian Carlo. AMAHL AND THE NIGHT VISITORS. Illustrated by Michele Lemieux. The story of the opera about a young boy and his gift to the Child.

Wojciechowski, Susan. THE CHRISTMAS MIRACLE OF JONATHAN TOOMEY. Illustrated by P. J. Lynch. Our favourite read-aloud Christmas story. A sad and gloomy woodcarver, through carving figures for a creche, finds the love and joy he had lost.

Godden, Rumer. THE STORY OF HOLLY AND IVY. Illustrated by Barbara Cooney. A wonderful little story in which all receive, in the end, what their hearts desire.

Pickthall, Marjorie. THE WORKER IN SANDALWOOD. Illustrated by Frances Tyrrell. *The* Carpenter helps a young apprentice accomplish an impossible task. A mythic and moving story of divine succour.

❧
Christmas Stories for the Older Child

Cooney, Caroline B. WHAT CHILD IS THIS? A CHRISTMAS STORY. Two foster children learn for the first time what Christmas is all about—and they hope, against all possibility, for the love of family. The chapters are headed with phrases from Christmas carols which draw subtle parallels between the Christmas story and the story of Matt and Katie.

Gaarder, Jostein. THE CHRISTMAS MYSTERY. Illustrated by Rosemary Wells. In a tiny shop, leaning against a wall of books, Joachim discovers a magic Advent calendar. As he opens the door for each day, we find ourselves with him in a rich, multi-leveled story perfect for reading one chapter at a time through Advent.

Paterson, Katherine. ANGELS AND OTHER STRANGERS. MIDNIGHT CLEAR. Two collections of stories the author has read over the years as a Christmas tradition in the church where her husband is the minister. These are stories for older children—and good to read aloud through Advent to inject freshness and richness into what God coming as a baby means in *real* life.

Robinson, Barbara. THE BEST CHRISTMAS PAGEANT EVER. A very funny and very profound story about what happened when some unsuitable children take over the annual Christmas pageant.

Van Dyke, Henry. THE STORY OF THE OTHER WISE MAN. This story is about the wise man who sought Jesus, but never found him— or so he thought. In the end he discovers, like Tolstoy's shoemaker, that he *has* found Jesus—as few ever do.

If you really read the fairy tales, you will observe that one idea runs from one end of them to the other—the idea that peace and happiness can only exist on some condition. This idea, which is the core of ethics, is the core of the nursery-tales.

—G.K. Chesterton

A novel, first of all, deals only indirectly with ideal forms or archetypes. Myths and fairy tales deal directly with archetypes, and there is a very real place for them, especially as they help children to map the dark regions of their souls, to face and conquer their inner dragons. We cannot, we must not, deprive children of these powerful images. Without them, not only do art and literature lose their power, but the soul itself stands ravaged and windowless like a vandalized cathedral.

—Katherine Paterson

. . . it is dangerous . . . [for the traveler in fairy-land] to ask too many questions, lest the gates should be shut and the keys be lost.

—J. R. R. Tolkien

7

Fairy Tales and Mythology

Fairy tales are the bones of Story. Sometimes we may know the name of a person who told the tale as it was recorded—such as Frau Viehmann, the "Fairy-tale wife" from whom the Grimm brothers gleaned many of their stories. But folk-tales, or what we refer to here as fairy tales, by definition have no identifiable author; they are an oral legacy handed down through the centuries. We use the term "Fantasy" for stories that are very like fairy tales, but for which we have an identifiable author. These more recent "fairy tales" are, however, often mere variations on tales which are rooted in "folk" stories—and their appeal and durability usually depend on that rooting.

Sometimes the old storytellers were wandering entertainers who travelled from place to place hearing stories and then re-telling and often re-tailoring them for avid listeners of all ages, not primarily children. Most often, however, they were the old women and men of a community. Though details gradually changed in their tellings, the basic thrust of many of the most well-known and well-loved of the tales is recognizable in widely-divergent cultures. "Cinderella," for example, has over 1500 versions, from places as scattered as Canada, Egypt and China, and recorded as early as 570 B.C.

Folktale heroes and heroines are everyman and everywoman—usually the downtrodden and abused of society—the cinder-ellas and cinder-lads of life who are in every tribe and town and who are part of the psyche of every person. We and our children find a deep satisfaction in these old stories because they are stories in which right and wrong—good and evil—are sharp and clear. Rewards go to the meek and lowly "-ellas" and "-lads"; punishment to the proud and domineering stepmothers and big sisters and brothers. Ultimate justice awaits all: the proud are scattered, the humble lifted up, and those without beauty—those who are "despised and rejected" by others, those who bear infirmities and carry sorrows—are "exalted to the highest place." The most enduring of these tales teach us the basic pattern and purpose of life, and these teachings help us face our dragons and keep our eyes on the glory.

The "Once Upon a Time . . ." or, "A very good time; not my time, not your time" (a story opening from the Bahamas), is all time and our time; the "Happily Ever After" is the victory of Hope over Despair. The land of fairy is a land of enchantment where anything can happen and fate can take strange twists and turns (the stories were usually told in those long night hours when all things seem possible). And yet that enchantment, that fate (both words are embedded in the etymology of "fairy"), those bones of fairy story have been honed by countless retellings to a skeletal frame that is sturdy enough to hold the flesh of our own needs and longings, our own hopes and dreams.

The best fairy stories ring true to our Christian faith because they are true not only to our own experience of life, but also to the Story that is at the heart of all truth. These stories tell over and over that help is available for anyone who is willing to request it—often from the humblest creatures. The good endings remind us of the Covenant, of God's promise of "a hope and a future" (Jeremiah 29:11). And yet Christian parents often try to protect their children from these stories.

Maybe such protection is appropriate for a *very* young child (though one young enough to need such protection probably wouldn't see the evil—or the good), but children—and *all* of us—need these stories to remind us that evil—and good—are very real. As Marcia Brown, a writer

90

of children's stories and reteller of folk tales has put it: "So much of living swings between the extremes of dark and light. The most honest books we can give our children do not tarnish the dazzle by obliterating the gloom."

Folk and fairy tales are both uncomfortably and comfortingly honest. They have a moral integrity that has been tried and tested and a spiritual integrity that we need in a culture where even the words "good" and "bad" are politically incorrect.

AESOP'S FABLES. Memorable and very wise little stories that should be part of every child's literary heritage.

Andersen, Hans Christian. ANDERSEN'S FAIRY TALES. Available in a variety of editions—the best, TWELVE TALES, retold and illustrated by Erik Blegvad, is currently out of print and difficult to find. Though technically these stories are not fairy tales in the "folk" sense in which we are using the term here, they still deserve to be in a child's storehouse of fairy tale memory since they draw deeply from the archetypes and motifs of folklore. A complete collection is HANS CHRISTIAN ANDERSEN: THE COMPLETE FAIRY TALES AND STORIES, translated by Erik Christian Haugaard. This wonderful tome includes Andersen's own notes for his stories and would be a good resource book for teachers and parents.

THE ARABIAN NIGHTS. Persian splendor in fine and fabulous tales that have given rich and haunting images to literature and life. Such familiar favourites as "Scheherazada," "Sinbad the Sailor," "Aladdin," and "Ali Baba and the Forty Thieves [Open, Sesame!]" should be part of every child's literary heritage.

Chase, Richard (collector and reteller). GRANDFATHER TALES. Famous and fun old tales from the southeast United States (North Carolina and Virginia)—tellings that derive mostly from England and Europe.

D'Aulaire, Ingri and Edgar Parin. BOOK OF GREEK MYTHS. NORSE GODS AND GODDESSES. Two whole cultural heritages, beautifully written and illustrated. EAST OF THE SUN AND WEST

OF THE MOON. An out-of-print collection of twenty-one Norwegian folktales that is well worth a search. Includes several Cinderlad (to balance "ella") stories.

Doherty, Berlie (reteller). FAIRY TALES. Illustrated by Jane Ray. A wonderful selection of favourite fairy tales, retold with verve and sparkle. The choice of favourite tales and the superb illustrations make for one of the best collections now available.

Finger, Charles (collector). TALES FROM SILVER LANDS. Newbery-winning book of Indian folk tales from South America.

Gag, Wanda. TALES FROM GRIMM. MORE TALES FROM GRIMM. Good retellings in the Grimm tradition and simple line illustrations that don't eliminate an imaginative picturing by the child.

Hamilton, Virginia. THE PEOPLE WHO COULD FLY. Illustrated by Leo and Diane Dillon. Folktales of the black southern United States which bring together a broad and rich heritage.

Harris, Christie. MOUSEWOMAN AND THE MISCHIEF-MAKERS. One of several of her books of Northwest Indian tales involving a mischievous mouse grandmother. THE TROUBLE WITH PRINCESSES. Northwest Indian tales of princesses, each prefaced by a comparison with similar tales from other countries.

Harris, Joel Chandler. JUMP! and JUMP AGAIN! Illustrated by Barry Moser. Two books on the adventures of Brer Rabbit, adapted by Van Dyke Parks from the original Uncle Remus stories.

Johnson, Pauline. LEGENDS OF VANCOUVER. West Coast Indian stories of the mythic mystery of British Columbia landmarks such as The Lions and Siwash Rock. Available in a new edition under her Indian name—Takahionwake.

Lang, Andrew. THE BLUE [RED, GRAY, PURPLE, PINK, BROWN, ETC.] FAIRY BOOK. Stories from all over the world, compiled and edited by this famous scholar of fairy tales. These are now available in a whole collection of reprints published by Dover Press that includes Pyle's THE WONDER CLOCK, Grimm's HOUSEHOLD TALES and THE JAPANESE FAIRY BOOK, compiled by Yei Theodora Ozaki. A new "sampler" of the colour fairy books is THE RAINBOW FAIRY BOOK, illustrated by Michael Hague.

Lanier, Sidney. THE BOY'S KING ARTHUR. Illustrated by N. C. Wyeth. A classic edition of these legends.

Mayol, Lurline Bowes. THE TALKING TOTEM POLE: THE TALES IT TOLD TO THE INDIAN CHILDREN OF THE NORTH-WEST. Ethically-strong stories, full of the scents and textures of the Northwest coast, told by the figures on an old totem pole to one twentieth-century native family. Worth hunting for.

Pilling, Ann. REALMS OF GOLD: MYTHS AND LEGENDS FROM AROUND THE WORLD. Illustrated by Kady MacDonald Denton. A collection of breadth and excellence in a format which keeps the stories unspoiled by over-illustration and yet accessible to younger children.

Pyle, Howard. THE MERRY ADVENTURES OF ROBIN HOOD. THE STORY OF KING ARTHUR AND HIS KNIGHTS. Well loved tellings of these old legends whose language suggests old English while remaining very readable. Also, in the same style, his own stories: OTTO OF THE SILVER HAND and THE WONDER CLOCK.

Seredy, Kate. THE WHITE STAG. The myth at the heart of the history of Hungary.

Sutcliff, Rosemary. THE WANDERINGS OF ODYSSEUS: THE STORY OF THE ODYSSEY. BLACK SHIPS BEFORE TROY. Both illustrated by Alan Lee. Stories from our Greek heritage of myth and legend written with Sutcliff's flair for using language in such a way as to make the past seem present.

Thomas, Gwyn and Kevin Crossley-Holland. TALES FROM THE MABINOGION. Illustrated by Margaret Jones. A fine edition for children of tales from the ancient Celtic heritage that is in the "genetic code" of Tolkien's LORD OF THE RINGS.

. . . Although now long estranged,
Man is not wholly lost nor wholly changed.
Dis-graced he may be, yet is not dethroned,
and keeps the rags of lordship once he owned:
Man, Sub-creator, the refracted Light
through whom is splintered from a single White
to many hues, and endlessly combined
in living shapes that move from mind to mind.
Though all the crannies of the world we filled
with Elves and Goblins, though we dared to build
Gods and their houses out of dark and light,
and sowed the seed of dragons—'twas our right
(used or misused). That right has not decayed:
we make still by the law in which we're made.
                                        —J. R. R. Tolkien

In very truth, a wise imagination, which is the presence
of the spirit of God, is the best guide that man or woman
can have; for it is not the things we see the most clearly
that influence us the most powerfully; undefined, yet
vivid visions of something beyond, something which eye
has not seen nor ear heard, have far more influence than
any logical sequences whereby the same things may be
demonstrated to the intellect. . . . We live by faith, and
not by sight.
                                        —George MacDonald

8

Fantasy and Science Fiction

Fantasy and science fiction give us a chance to explore the dark and bright aspects of the human mind, soul, and heart. Archetypes, imagery, and the vehicles of Fairy Tale and Journey take us to another land or time and then return us to our own everyday lives with a renewed sense of what it means to be human. Ursula K. Le Guin writes:

> We read books to find out who we are. What other people, real or imaginary, do and think and feel—or have done and thought and felt; or might do and think and feel—is an essential guide to our understanding of what we ourselves are and may become . . . a person who had never listened to nor read a tale nor myth or parable or story, would remain ignorant of his own emotional and spiritual heights and depths, would not know quite fully what it is to be human.

Through fantasy and science fiction we are provided a place where strong feelings and deep issues can be discussed without having to be watered down or contextualized in our present culture. For example, the bullying which Eustace Scrubb experiences in THE SILVER CHAIR is ended by a roaring lion (and warriors with swords and riding whips) trouncing and terrifying the bullies. Unrealistic, but satisfying. And per-haps—for the bullied child—empowering.

Speculation and "what-ifs" are a large part of fantasy and science fiction. What if I had a toy cupboard that made everything I put into it real? What if the clock really *did* strike thirteen times? Some authors have used fairly pleasant what-ifs as a start to a story, but many have speculated about present day problems and exaggerated them. What if we *could* live forever? What if we ran out of space and energy on Earth?

These genres are often written off as "escape literature," and in truth we often travel to fantastic places! But in the great works, as in all genres, we return from the journey all the wiser.

Alexander, Lloyd. THE BOOK OF THREE. The first of the Chronicles of Prydain, a Welsh mythic kingdom. TIME CAT. A boy and a cat take part in great moments of history. THE FOUNDLING AND OTHER STORIES OF PRYDAIN. "The Foundling" is a particu-larly moving story of the place of life's experiences in maturity and old age.

Almond, David. SKELLIG. Michael finds a strange creature who likes to eat flies and Chinese take-out; who has mysterious, birdlike lumps on his shoulders; and who possibly holds the key to healing Michael's baby sister.

Babbit, Natalie. TUCK EVERLASTING. About the good and the bad of *not* being able to grow old.

Banks, Lynne Reid. THE INDIAN IN THE CUPBOARD. THE RE-TURN OF THE INDIAN. And lots of sequels. Fun, light-hearted books with some good underlying lessons on integrity and compas-sion.

Bond, Nancy. A STRING IN THE HARP. A strong, memorable story in which the members of a very real family, struggling to recover from the death of the mother, rent an old house on the coast of Wales and find an ancient harp-tuning key that brings them into contact with the life and music of that fine old bard of TALES FROM THE MABINOGION, Taliesin.

Boston, Lucy. THE CHILDREN OF GREENE KNOWE. The first of a series of books in which the children of eight centuries find each other in a *real* house (the oldest continuously occupied house in Britain—and, until she died, the home of Lucy Boston).

Briggs, K. M. HOBBERDY DICK. Stories of the little hobgoblins that used to (and maybe still do!) haunt our houses—or at least the manors of England.

Christopher, John. THE WHITE MOUNTAINS. THE CITY OF GOLD AND LEAD. THE POOL OF FIRE. A trilogy which tells the story of a group of boys who join a band of men trying to overthrow an alien power which has gained control of the earth by controlling people's minds.

Clark, Catherine Anthony. THE GOLDEN PINE CONE. Firmly set in the Kootenays and Indian lore of British Columbia, this classic marks the beginning of Canadian fantasy for children. Recently republished, which is wonderful, but find an old edition for worthy illustrations by Claire Bice.

Farmer, Nancy. THE EAR, THE EYE AND THE ARM. A story of three sheltered children on a boy scout adventure gone awry in a futuristic African city. Parents who are squeamish about pseudo-spiritual elements might want to pre-read this book.

Gannett, Ruth Stiles. MY FATHER'S DRAGON. In this book suitable for a younger reader, a small boy sets out with only his wits and a carefully-loaded backpack (including twenty-five peanut butter and jelly sandwiches) to rescue a small dragon held captive on Wild Island.

Hoover, H. M. THE DELIKON. THIS TIME OF DARKNESS. And many others. Science fiction books rich in good writing and good values with strong women as heroes.

Hughes, Monica. KEEPER OF THE ISIS LIGHT. GUARDIAN OF ISIS. THE TOMORROW CITY. And *many* others. KEEPER and GUARDIAN are the best of Hughes's books, but all of them make interesting reading. Strange future settings—but familiar problems and prejudices considered wisely from the perspective of this Canadian author.

Hunter, Mollie. THE HAUNTED MOUNTAIN. A superb, suspenseful fantasy folk story. A STRANGER CAME ASHORE draws on the bittersweet Scottish tales of the Selkie or seal people of the sea.

Jacques, Brian. REDWALL. And numerous sequels. Epic adventure, noble quests, and courageous deeds fill these tales of the mice of Redwall Abbey. CASTAWAYS OF THE FLYING DUTCHMAN. During a wild wintry voyage around Cape Horn, a boy and his dog are washed from the deck of the ill-fated Flying Dutchman. In their wanderings through the centuries to come, they bring hope and healing to needy folks and especially to the threatened town of Chapelvale.

Kendall, Carol. THE GAMMAGE CUP. Wonderful story of an eccentric group of people who save their village. The Minnipins live along the river in the Land Between the Mountains. They wear green cloaks and paint their doors green. All except for "the others," who wear *bright* cloaks and paint their doors vibrant colours; instead of having proper jobs, they paint, write poetry, and dig for buried treasure. But *they* are the ones who find out about the invasion through the mountains and who come up with a scheme to save the village.

L'Engle, Madeleine. A WRINKLE IN TIME. RING OF ENDLESS LIGHT. Two of the *many* books by this award-winning author. Brilliant children act heroically in a setting that skillfully blends fantasy, science fiction, and ordinary life.

Le Guin, Ursula K. THE WIZARD OF EARTHSEA. THE TOMBS OF ATUAN. Both of these books are set in Earthsea. They are profound in their psychological insight and superb in story. These first two of the series are the best. Don't give up halfway through TOMBS;

it is a story in which the "darkness of the gloom" is finally dispelled by the "dazzle of the glory" (Marcia Brown). THE FARTHEST SHORE and TEHANU complete the "Earthsea" series. They are good adult reading, but much darker.

Lewis, C. S. THE LION, THE WITCH AND THE WARDROBE. The first written of the seven books in The Chronicles of Narnia (though THE MAGICIANS NEPHEW is first in Narnia's history). The series is perhaps the most perfect example in the twentieth century of stories which embody the Good News in all the pagan richness of European legend and mythology without compromising the Story. Many read it with no knowledge of its Christian dimension. But who knows how many people have come to love Jesus because they first came to love the great lion Aslan? The series includes THE HORSE AND HIS BOY, PRINCE CASPIAN, THE VOYAGE OF THE DAWNTREADER, THE SILVER CHAIR, and THE LAST BATTLE. All great for reading aloud, repeatedly, to a wide age span.

Lively, Penelope. THE GHOST OF THOMAS KEMPE. THE HOUSE AT NORHAM GARDENS. In both of these books the modern main characters experience the past as real and, in thus discovering the continuity of past and present, gain understanding and insight for living in the present.

Lowry, Lois. THE GIVER. In a seemingly ideal society where nothing is wasted and everyone is employed, Jonas is assigned to be the next Receiver of Memory—the person who holds all the memories of the past for his society. Jonas is made aware of the deep problems in his society and, with the Giver of Memories, he starts to plan a way to change things. Lois Lowry manages to deal with problems and keep a wholesomeness of perspective. A fine and thought-provoking book that is in itself a commentary on contemporary life, even though the setting is far (or maybe not so far) in the future. GATHERING BLUE. Another futuristic setting for a very different society ruled by violence and cruelty in which Kira, a crippled girl with an artist's gift, is barely surviving.

Lunn, Janet. THE ROOT CELLAR. Discover the 1800's in an Ontario cellar. SHADOW IN HAWTHORN BAY. "Second sight" in an eerily beautiful story of a girl from Scotland who settles in Canada.

MacDonald, George. THE PRINCESS AND THE GOBLIN. THE PRINCESS AND CURDIE. Should be part of every child's read-aloud heritage—well worth waiting for the right time. Two editions of GOBLIN by classic illustrators are excellent: Morrow Junior Books with illustrations by Jessie Wilcox Smith, and Random House with the original illustrator, Arthur Hughes. *And,* try to find a good, *unabridged* collection of his FAIRY STORIES.

McKinley, Robin. BEAUTY. ROSE DAUGHTER. SPINDLE'S END. The first is a novel-length retelling of "Beauty and the Beast" that follows the traditional tale. The second was written twenty years later and moves farther from the traditional tale without ruining the beauty of the story (even with the addition of unicorn manure). The third is a novel-length retelling and adaptation of "Sleeping Beauty."

Murphy, Shirley Rousseau. SILVER WOVEN IN MY HAIR. A "Cinderella" story about a Cinderella who gives us thoughtful commentary and background on Cinderella stories—and who writes one herself.

Nesbit, E. THE ENCHANTED CASTLE. THE RAILWAY CHILDREN. And others, all of which have been favourites with English-speaking children for a long time. These are fantasies in the lives of active children.

O'Brien, Robert C. MRS. FRISBY AND THE RATS OF NIMH. Through the experiments of a research station, a community of rats has become extremely intelligent. They use their wisdom to help the mouse widow of Mr. Frisby who was tragically involved in one of the research projects.

Park, Ruth. PLAYING BEATTIE BOW. A top-notch historical fantasy of time-travel and romance, set in Sydney, Australia.

Paterson, Katherine. THE KING'S EQUAL. Illustrated by Vladimir Vagin. In a brilliant switch of our expectations (and his!), a prince finds that he cannot marry the girl who suits him until he is her equal— and so has to learn what we recognize as the basic lessons of care, trustworthiness and love. A "young" enough book to be an "old" picture book.

Pearce, A. Phillippa. TOM'S MIDNIGHT GARDEN. A classic fantasy in which Tom comes to terms with his present through midnight encounters with his family's past.

Pearson, Kit. AWAKE AND DREAMING. Theo has grown up the neglected daughter of Rae, a young, unwed mother. When Rae ships her to Victoria, Theo imagines herself into the lives of a wonderful family with lots of love, books, toys, food, patience, and pets. When she comes out of this "dream phase," she finds herself trying desperately to return to it. This is a fascinating book which includes the ghost of a children's book writer. It doesn't provide trite and simple answers, like so many novels about unhappy children. Theo realizes that she is not the only one with an unhappy family: a friend at school is missing her father as her mother starts a new life with her female partner.

Pope, Elizabeth. THE PERILOUS GARD. A medieval setting for a story of mystery, romance, fantasy and profoundly Christian imagery, with a depth to warrant many re-readings.

Richler, Mordecai. JACOB TWO-TWO MEETS THE HOODED FANG. First in a series of "Jacob" fantasy stories by a Canadian novelist. Slapstick and scary.

Rowling, J. K. HARRY POTTER AND THE PHILOSOPHER'S STONE. After growing up as a despised orphan nephew in his aunt and uncle's house, Harry Potter is enrolled and sent off to Hogwart's School of Witchcraft and Wizardry. With many references to typical English boarding schools, this book turns into a funny, magical adventure story—enjoyable even for "Muggles" like us. And SEQUELS! They get better and better, according to many fans, and are the first children's books to places 1, 2, 3 and 4 on the adult bestseller list. (See "Parental Guidance" in **Helps Along the Way to Good Books for Children.**)

Sandburg, Carl. ROOTABAGAS. MORE ROOTABAGAS. New editions of these homey fantasies are available now, illustrated by Paul Zelinsky—a perfect matchup. The ROOTABAGA stories are the source for that wonderful bedtime story, THE WEDDING PROCESSION OF THE RAG DOLL AND THE BROOM HANDLE AND WHO WAS IN IT. (See "Goodnight Books" in **Picture Books.)**

Thornton, Duncan. KALIFAX. The wild northern adventure of a ship and her crew caught for the winter in the grip of ice and snow. With courage and perseverance, young Tom braves the elements, is rescued by Grandfather Frost, and saves the ship. The words are stretching and wonderful, and the illustrations by Yves Noblet capture the mythic wildness of the story.

Tolkien, J. R. R. THE HOBBIT. THE LORD OF THE RINGS (3 volumes). The greatest fantasy, and the best book (next to the BIBLE) ever written. Absolutely superb to read over and over and over— **aloud**! The Christian dimensions are less obvious than in Lewis's Narnia books—but are perhaps even more foundational to the very shape of the story.

White, T. H. MISTRESS MASHAM'S REPOSE. An eccentric professor and a little girl "help" some stranded Lilliputians.

Wrightson, Patricia. THE NARGUN AND THE STARS. A LITTLE FEAR. Books which bring wonderfully ordinary people up against the primal spirits of Australian mythology.

Wyndham, John. THE CHRYSALIDS. Takes place in the future, many generations after a nuclear holocaust. Society is slowly rebuilding, aided in part by a strict, religiously-applied definition of "human." David, whose father is the local minister and primary enforcer of biological orthodoxy, discovers that he and some of his friends have the ability to communicate telepathically, and many difficult questions follow.

Tipsy bear's rotundity, toad's complacence . . .
Why! they all cry out to be used as symbols,
Masks for Man, cartoons, parodies by Nature
       Formed to reveal us

Each to each, not fiercely but in her gentlest
       Vein of household laughter.
                        —C.S. Lewis

9

Animal Stories

Animal stories have always been a trademark of children's literature—at least until Richard Adams' WATERSHIP DOWN appeared to defy all classifications of type or age. Both WATERSHIP DOWN and Adams' second "animal book," THE PLAGUE DOGS, are superb exemplars of the continuing appeal and goodness of the animal story—for all of us, adults and children alike. Since such stories make animals seem human, we become aware of the hurts and anxieties, excitements and joys of an "other" being. Sometimes also, in the very highest sense, they make humans seem animal, and thus help us better understand the depth and mystery of our creatureliness.

After reading THE PLAGUE DOGS or BAMBI (Felix Salten's story, not Disney's) or CHARLOTTE'S WEB we know an important and deeply Christian principle—that all God's creation and creatures deserve our respect and understanding, our consideration and care. That empathy with the non-human but fully sentient (at least in these books!) dogs, deer and spiders of these stories allows us to explore our *own* inner world freely and fully—without any need to measure ourselves by some other, often intimidating, real-life human character. In THE WIND IN THE WIL-

LOWS (perhaps the greatest of animal stories) we can be insecure Mole, who is ashamed of his simple, shabby (i.e. well-used) home—or his friend, thoughtful Rat, who gently and inobtrusively helps him see his richness of home and friends. Or we can be pompous Toad! We live the life of each.

In putting on the masks of these animal beings we are more able to take off our own masks of false humility or bravado. What is even more important, we grow in our ability to see through each mask of those around us to the real person hiding underneath.

Animal Realism (at least relatively)

Branford, Henrietta. FIRE, BED, AND BONE. A dog's story about life for herself and her pups, as well as her master, his family, the village, and the countryside around them in the years of the Peasants' Revolt of the 1300's.

Burnford, Sheila. THE INCREDIBLE JOURNEY. An incredible animal survival story: the poignant, hard-won reuniting of animals with their beloved owner.

Grey Owl (also known as George Stansfeld Belaney). SAJO AND THE BEAVER PEOPLE. A Canadian classic about two children who help two beavers.

Haig-Brown, Roderick. PANTHER. (Previously KI-YU.) A cougar-hunt story set in the wilderness of Vancouver Island, British Columbia, gives a naturalist's understanding of cougars and of the place.

Henry, Marguerite. KING OF THE WIND. Based on the legendary history of the father of Arabian horses and his mute trainer. One of (and the best of) many fine Henry horse stories—most of which are based on some fact.

Mowat, Farley. OWLS IN THE FAMILY. THE DOG THAT WOULDN'T BE. Mowat's rather unbelievable and hilariously funny animal stories continue to be great favourites with Canadian children—and adults.

O'Neill, Mary. THE WHITE PALACE. The life story of Chinoo, a Chinook Salmon. Conveys sensitivity to the meaning of life—and death.

Rawlings, Marjorie Kinnan. THE YEARLING. Illustrated by N. C. Wyeth. A classic story of hunting, horses, farmlife and boyhood.

Roberts, Sir Charles G. D. SEVEN BEARS. RED FOX. Real-life stories by a Canadian naturalist. RED FOX is great writing, an education, a moving story and, in spite of the Disney juxtaposition of hair-raising events, a piece of credible realism. The excellent line-drawing illustrations are by John Schoenherr.

Salten, Felix. BAMBI. (*Not* the Disney version) Through many years, a dear deer story.

Seton, Ernest Thompson. WILD ANIMALS I HAVE KNOWN. Written from a naturalist-hunter's point of view.

Sewell, Anna. BLACK BEAUTY. One of the first great animal stories. Comes down hard and vividly on cruelty to animals, but the sadness of such actions is balanced by the overwhelming joy of restoration—and rest—at the end. A powerful book. Available in a fine edition illustrated by Charles Keeping.

Animal Fantasy

Alexander, Lloyd. THE CAT WHO WISHED TO BE A MAN. The cat gets his wish and *we* learn much about what it means—or should mean—to be human. TIME CAT. An interplay of humans and cats down through history.

Atwater, Richard and Florence. MR. POPPER'S PENGUINS. A story of the comic perplexities Mr. Popper must solve when he receives a houseful of penguins.

Grahame, Kenneth. THE WIND IN THE WILLOWS. THE RELUCTANT DRAGON. Both of these books have the feel of myth and describe characters (such as Toad) and places (such as Badger's burrow) in such a way as to leave us with understanding and longing. WIND IN THE WILLOWS should be read aloud to become a shared, savored experience.

King-Smith, Dick. BABE: THE GALLANT PIG. A pig aspires and works hard to *be* a sheepdog! Good fun. THE HODGEHEG. A shocked hedgehog gets everything mixed up in his attempt to figure out traffic safety.

Kipling, Rudyard. THE JUNGLE BOOK. Mowgli, a human boy, is raised and protected by his wolf family and jungle friends. See also his JUST SO STORIES which tell you, among other such "facts," how the elephant got his long nose.

Milne, A. A. WINNIE THE POOH. THE HOUSE AT POOH CORNER. Illustrated by Ernest Shepard. Tiddely Pom! Philosophy and psychology tucked in every nook of these books about Christopher Robin and his friends Pooh, Eeyore, Tigger, Piglet and the rest.

White, E. B. CHARLOTTE'S WEB. THE TRUMPET OF THE SWAN. STUART LITTLE. Blends of naturalist detail and wisdom. CHARLOTTE'S WEB is one of the finest books in all of children's literature.

I feel it to be enormously important that the young should be given this sense of continuity, that they should be given the feeling of their roots behind them. To know and really understand something of where one comes from helps one to understand and cope better with where one is now—and where one is going to. And as we today are standing too near our own particular stretch of history to be able to make out the pattern and "see how the story ends," so I feel that history can best be brought to life for children through people in the like situation with regard to their own stretch of history, people standing too close to see the pattern, and who, like us, "don't know how the story ends."

—Rosemary Sutcliff

To be unaware of a sense of continuity is to be affected by a kind of paralysis of the imagination. . . . To help a child see himself as part of a whole historical perspective is to extend his imagination. Without such awareness he is blinkered, confined by self, and dangerous.

—Penelope Lively

And the end of all our exploring
Will be to arrive where we started
And know the place for the first time.

—T. S. Eliot

10

Historical Fiction

One of the sins of which we moderns stand rightly accused is chronological snobbery: we assume that our own time and ideas are the best just because they are most recent. Probably human beings throughout time have always assumed that their own ways and means, technologies and beliefs are the best. But without doubt our own time outranks all others in its assumption of superiority: we know more and we know better. Such snobbery not only lacks an understanding of the innovative creativity at the heart of any human process; it also extends automatically to cultural snobbery, religious snobbery, and what we could call *expertise* snobbery (i.e., my particular training, specialization or vocation has the clearest insights).

Historical fiction undermines such snobbery in two ways. It creates an intellectual curiosity about the past and consequently an appreciation for (if not amazement at) the skill and ingenuity of the peoples of the past. Consider, for example, the art of sailing: reading Patrick O'Brian's sea stories will squelch any feeling that the old sea captains such as Jack Aubrey were in any intellectual, cultural, or technological way less advanced. Jack knew the sea and the winds better than anyone who depends on motors to solve dilemmas.

Good historical fiction's best contribution, however, is to make us aware of a continuity that is more than historical. Historical fiction reinforces what the Bible teaches us over and over: that, as the author of Ecclesiastes puts it (Ecclesiastes 1:9):

> What has been will be again,
>> What has been done will be done again,
>> there is nothing new under the sun.

Throughout human history men and women have loved and hated—and felt the wonder of being alive in a mysterious, terrible and wonderful world. *Always*, men and women have struggled, as Rosemary Sutcliff puts it, in "doing the right/kind/brave/honest thing." To be most fully human, we need to love good, hate evil, and understand the struggle between the two—in ourselves, and in others. And we are immeasurably helped by stories of people in other times, stories which make us feel and know that this struggle is a very old one and that there is hope.

Some of the books in this section are loose fits—technically they might be considered autobiography or fictionalized biography, or even realistic fiction about a distant (in more ways than years or miles) culture.

Bishop, Claire Hutchet. TWENTY AND TEN. French children show courage and care in protecting ten Jewish children from Nazi deportation.

Carter, Forrest. THE EDUCATION OF LITTLE TREE. Little Tree is raised with integrity in the mountains by his immensely loving Cherokee grandparents. He learns about whisky-making, hunting, and harvesting the woods. This is Forrest Carter's profoundly beautiful remembrance of his grandparents.

Clark, Ann Nolan. SECRET OF THE ANDES. An Inca boy discovers his people's rich past.

Edmonds, Walter D. THE MATCHLOCK GUN. Young Edward courageously protects his family during an Indian raid in the 1700's on the American frontier.

Forbes, Esther. JOHNNY TREMAIN. A classic, Newbery-winning story of life in the American colonies. The Revolutionary War transforms Johnny from a cocky youngster to a mature citizen of the new country.

Gray, Elizabeth Janet. ADAM OF THE ROAD. Young Adam, son of Roger the minstrel, gets separated from his father and his beloved spaniel. His travels and adventures teach both him and us much about the realities of life and human character in medieval England.

Gardiner, John. STONE FOX. A young boy, his dog, and an old Indian man together win a dogsled race. This is a book about the potential greatness of the human spirit.

Garfield, Leon. SMITH. Typical of Garfield—some mystery, some background history—but mostly an exciting adventure story.

Haig-Brown, Roderick. THE WHALE PEOPLE. A Northwest Indian boy learns to hunt whales.

Hautzig, Esther. THE ENDLESS STEPPE. A Jewish family is deported to Siberia—based on the life of the author. A story of determination and resilience as they not only *endure*, but learn to love the beauty of that lonely landscape.

Hawes, Charles Boardman. THE DARK FRIGATE. A sea adventure story about Philip Marsham, a young boy who is caught by and made part of a pirate crew and consequently has to struggle for his personal integrity and for his life.

Hesse, Karen. OUT OF THE DUST. Set in the Oklahoma Dust Bowl of the Great Depression. Billie Jo copes with dust, the tragic death of her mother and baby brother, and burns which cripple her hands. The book is written in a series of free verse poems. Some of the sentiments about the land and responsible farming practices seem to be from a more contemporary mindset, but they don't overpower the book.

Hughes, Monica. BLAINE'S WAY. A "growing up" story—and a love story—about a boy who takes part in World War II.

Kogawa, Joy. NAOMI'S ROAD. A short, children's version of OBA-SAN, the story of a British Columbia Japanese-Canadian family in World War II, when to be Japanese meant to be an enemy.

Latham, Jean Lee. CARRY ON, MR. BOWDITCH. Based on the true story of Nathaniel Bowditch who, on his own, with little chance for schooling, mastered the mathematics of nautical navigation. He went on to become captain of his own ship and writer of a textbook used by navigators for over one hundred years.

Lenski, Lois. INDIAN CAPTIVE: THE STORY OF MARY JEMISON. Includes talks with Indian descendants of Mary Jemison, "White Woman of the Genessee." The book presents the harsh realities of frontier tensions, as well as a respect for the values and good qualities of quite different cultures—"Indian" and "White."

Little, Jean. HIS BANNER OVER ME. The fictionalized biography of Jean Little's grandmother's life as the daughter of missionaries to China. A good book in which she not only reveals the agonies and problems of separation from family which characterized the lives of many early missionaries, but also enriches our sense of those great struggles by carefully chosen words from old hymns and songs of the Christian faith. LITTLE BY LITTLE and STARS COME OUT WITHIN. Not fiction, but her own stories of struggling with increasingly poor eyesight and longings to write.

Lowry, Lois. NUMBER THE STARS. Annemarie and her Danish family take on the risk of helping her friend, Ellen, and *her* Jewish family go "underground" to the safety of Sweden.

MacLachlan, Patricia. SARAH, PLAIN AND TALL. The longing of two pioneer children for a new mother. Only fifty-eight pages of big print, but rich in characterization. *Try* to stay away from the video, which trivializes, distorts and, for ever after, ruins this finely-honed gem of a book.

McLaughrean, Geraldine. A LITTLE LOWER THAN THE ANGELS. Gabriel is a survivor. After surviving—and escaping from—a cruel stonemason, he joins a traveling group of mystery players and survives squabbles, hunger, and the plague.

Martel, Suzanne. THE KING'S DAUGHTER. A Canadian backwoodsman orders a bride from France.

Morpurgo, Michael. TWIST OF GOLD. Set in the desperate exodus from Ireland during the potato famine. WAR HORSE. A World War I story told from the viewpoint of a cavalry horse. WAITING FOR ANYA. Tells the story of Jo, a French boy who, through his own curiousity, is drawn into helping hide Jewish children before they sneak over the border into Spain. Morpurgo tells the story with a sense of the tension that comes from having to keep a secret for years.

O'Dell, Scott. ISLAND OF THE BLUE DOLPHINS. A girl/woman lives for many years alone on an island in the Pacific. She struggles to stay alive, both physically and emotionally, and gradually gains strength and endurance in body, soul and mind. Is—and richly deserves to be—a classic.

Paterson, Katherine. LYDDIE. A factory girl has to choose between marrying or finishing her education. The conflict may be more modern than the setting of the book would allow; still, it points out a life choice that many girls face in late adolescence. JIP: HIS STORY. The struggles of Jip give a keen sense of the narrow gap that lay between safety and slavery, between security and integrity in the mid 1800's. A gripping story that renews faith in the strength of friendship and compassion.

Pearson, Kit. THE SKY IS FALLING. Norah and Gavin are sent to Canada to be protected from the constant bombing of England in 1940. The book is not only a "good read," but shows how adjusting to new places and people goes hand in hand with understanding. The first of a trilogy.

Propp, Vera. WHEN THE SOLDIERS WERE GONE. Based on the true story of a Jewish boy who spent the German occupation of Holland on a farm with Christians. When his Jewish parents come to pick him up after the war, he has no memory of them, his Judaism, or his name, and he must adjust to a life he has forgotten. This story is told in simple language, but the subject matter would be just as appropriate for an older reader.

Richter, Conrad. THE LIGHT IN THE FOREST. A young white boy, reared as an Indian after capture at the age of four, must make the hard choice between his real parents and his close-knit Indian family.

Schmidt, Gary D. ANSON'S WAY. Anson joins his father as part of the British troops sent to keep the Irish in line during the 18th century. He quickly becomes disillusioned with both the means and the reasons that his father's troops employ, while at the same time becoming fascinated with the Irish countryside, the Irish hedgerow teacher he meets, and the perseverence of the Irish people under persecution.

Serralier, Ian. ESCAPE FROM WARSAW. (Also titled THE SILVER SWORD.) Three children are separated from their parents during the war, and finally, after much pluck and luck, are reunited.

Smucker, Barbara. UNDERGROUND TO CANADA. A Canadian historical fiction classic about the underground "railway" for bringing black slaves from the southern States to freedom in Canada. See also DAYS OF TERROR (about a Mennonite boy leaving Russia) and AMISH ADVENTURE.

Speare, Elizabeth. THE WITCH OF BLACKBIRD POND. About a witch hunt in New England and the insight that comes into who is *really* hurting others. THE BRONZE BOW. Set in the days of the New Testament. THE SIGN OF THE BEAVER. A pioneer boy learns to live on his own with the help of an Indian friend. CALICO CAPTIVE. Another Pioneer story. Speare did not write much, but every book she wrote is fine literature and has won awards. In 1989 she won the Hans Christian Anderson Award for the whole body of her work.

Sperry, Armstrong. CALL IT COURAGE. Young Mufatu lives on an island of the South Seas, but struggles with a great fear of the sea. He sets out on a voyage to conquer that fear and comes home weak in body but strong in spirit.

Staples, Suzanne Fisher. SHABANU: DAUGHTER OF THE WIND. Technically a realistic book of desert life in Pakistan—in a society, however, that is quickly becoming history. A young Muslim girl struggles between her own longings and her love for her family and her respect for tradition. This book forces us to live in her world, feel the agony of her conflicts and consequently struggle with her in her questions. HAVALI. The sequel, in which Shabanu struggles with her marriage. Both these books open a new world to us—but the portrayal of that world is still much more western in ideas, goals and presumptions than her world would have been in real life.

Sutcliff, Rosemary. WARRIOR SCARLET. THE EAGLE OF THE NINTH. THE SHIELD RING. THE LANTERN BEARERS. DAWN WIND. THE SILVER BRANCH. SUN HORSE, MOON HORSE. (And many others.) Fine, richly-woven stories bring British history to life—particularly the centuries-long waves of invasions (Celtic, Roman, Saxon, Norman) which produced the language, literature, and culture of the British Isles. We think Sutcliff is the very best of historical novelists—we re-read her books endlessly.

Wilder, Laura Ingalls. LITTLE HOUSE IN THE BIG WOODS. Start at the *beginning*, with this book, and read through the whole wonderful series of the *real* LITTLE HOUSE books—time a family vacation to South Dakota and Minnesota towards the end and see where it all happened. Beware! Some widely advertised, supposed "more little house" books that have nothing to do with Wilder and the solid family historical base she used for her writing are trying to tag on to the continuing great love readers have for the originals.

Watkins, Yoko Kawashima. SO FAR FROM THE BAMBOO GROVE. MY BROTHER, MY SISTER AND I. These books are Yoko Watkins's own story of her escape, as a Japanese foreigner, from Korea during WWII, her survival in post-war Japan and a brief account of her coming to live in the States. A warm, heartening, courageous set of books through which shine her goodness and loyalty and love.

Wojciechowska, Maia. I, JUAN DE PAREJA. This story of the great Spanish painter Velasquez gives us not only human understanding, but artistic insight.

Yates, Elizabeth. AMOS FORTUNE, FREE MAN. The life-story of a black man of great integrity, fortitude and generosity—one of those books that sets a standard for character and commitment in life. Based on the life of a former slave buried in the churchyard cemetery of Jaffrey, New Hampshire.

Yolen, Jane. THE DEVIL'S ARITHMETIC. A holocaust historical fantasy framed by the ritual open door of the Seder Supper and focused on the need to *remember*. (BRIAR ROSE, also by Yolen, is an adult parallel that uses the Sleeping Beauty folktale as its structural motif.)

He ate and drank the precious Words—
His spirit grew robust—
He knew no more that he was poor,
Nor that his frame was Dust—

He danced along the dingy Days
And this Bequest of Wings
Was but a Book—What Liberty
A loosened spirit brings—

—Emily Dickinson

A truly great book should be read in youth, again in maturity and once more in old age.

—Robertson Davies

A classic is a book that has never finished saying what it has to say.

—Italo Calvino

11

Good Stories

"Good stories" is a definition in itself, but to clarify your understanding we offer a quote from a reader, a librarian and a children's book
writer: Kit Pearson. Pearson is describing Theo, the main character of her
novel AWAKE AND DREAMING:

> Choosing a new book was like looking for treasure. Theo
> always took a good long time. First she examined some paperbacks on
> a revolving stand. But they were mostly novels about one girl or one
> boy with a problem, or horror stories with scary covers. That wasn't
> what she wanted.
>
> She knew she'd have better luck on the shelves where the
> older hardcover books were kept. She walked along looking at them
> slowly, tilting her head to read the titles. *Half Magic, The Moffats, The
> Family from One End Street* . . . Theo tingled with pleasure as she
> recognized favourites from other libraries.
>
> At her last school there had been only paperbacks. But this
> new library was the best kind—it didn't throw out its old books. They
> looked ugly, with their thick, plain covers. But the dull outsides
> concealed the best stories.

Usually a title would leap out at her, as if it were shouting, "Read *me!*" And here it was—*All-of-a-Kind Family.* Theo pulled it off the shelf. The cover was sturdy and green, with a faded picture on it. It showed five girls in matching old-fashioned dresses and pinafores tumbling down some stairs. They were all smiling and, best of all, they were holding books!

Theo opened it up, read the enticing first sentence, then sighed with relief. She'd found the right book.

In this chapter, "Old Favourites" are those old books whose "dull outsides concealed the best stories." They have been favourites for generations. "New Favourites" may still be "paperbacks on a revolving stand," and some may even be "about one girl or one boy with a problem," but we *think* these will be with the "best stories" lingering on the back shelves another generation or two from now. "Adventures" are more exciting than many of the other favourites, with action emphasized more than the inner life of the characters.

Whichever one or ones you choose, we hope you also, with a sigh of relief, find the right book.

❧

Old Favourites

Alcott, Louisa May. LITTLE WOMEN. A classic and beautiful old story of girlhood, family life, and romance. Alcott fans will find that her other books, such as LITTLE MEN and ROSE IN BLOOM, are rich lodes of good reading.

Armstrong, William. SOUNDER. The story of a southern black family torn apart by poverty and prejudice. The sadness of the story works resolutely through deep grief to a bittersweet but powerfully-good ending. SOURLAND. Another sad but deeply good book that is actually a sequel.

Brink, Carol Ryrie. CADDIE WOODLAWN. A deeply-satisfying read for any tomboy who loves the country.

Bunyan, John. PILGRIM'S PROGRESS. An old book that somehow still speaks to modern readers about the ups and downs of the Christian life. Though retellings of such classics often cheapen originals, Gary D. Schmidt of Calvin College has redone the story in such a way that not only makes it more accessible for the modern reader, but also, especially with Barry Moser's superb illustrations, reinvigorates the imagination with fresh insights. Unfortunately, however, the Christiana section was not redone, and though not well known, it is an important part of the whole story. The original version works amazingly well as a read-aloud.

Burnett, Frances Hodgson. THE SECRET GARDEN. THE LITTLE PRINCESS. THE LOST PRINCE. These old favourites combine the material for perfect stories—gardens no one has gone into for many years, orphans, mean cooks, diamond mines, a prince in hiding, etc.—with a desire to convey whatever is good and pure and noble.

Carroll, Lewis. ALICE'S ADVENTURES IN WONDERLAND and THROUGH THE LOOKING-GLASS. Whimsically fantastical—and a literary legacy. One of those books that profits from being read aloud.

Dodge, Mary Maples. HANS BRINKER OR THE SILVER SKATES. A warmly satisfying story of the caring and courage of a Dutch family in the face of poverty and tragedy. Full of detail of Dutch life in the 1800's. One of those books that is well worth reading aloud if that's the only way you can "make it go down."

Enright, Elizabeth. THIMBLE SUMMER (Newbery winner). GONE-AWAY LAKE. Calm and comfortable—and comforting—stories of childhood in the 50's.

Goudge, Elizabeth. LINNETS AND VALERIANS. One of many children's books by this famous English author. Solid in storytelling and in the truths of life. THE LITTLE WHITE HORSE. A perfect story on the borderline between English historical fiction and fairy tale (Carnegie Medal, 1946—England). These books are hard to find (though the latter is now available in paperback), but they are well worth the search. SMOKY HOUSE. A magical, silver-spun story of smugglers, secrets and the stuff of good dreams—and, therefore, even harder to find.

MacDonald, George. SIR GIBBIE. Edited by Elizabeth Yates. A *good* story about a mute boy in Scotland—an excellent read-aloud. THE PRINCESS AND THE GOBLIN. THE PRINCESS AND CURDIE. See also his fairy tales.

McCloskey, Robert. HOMER PRICE and CENTERBURG TALES. Delightfully unrealistic stories of Homer Price and the other quirky citizens of Centerburg.

Montgomery, Lucy M. ANNE OF GREEN GABLES. EMILY OF NEW MOON. PAT OF SILVER BUSH. THE BLUE CASTLE. JANE OF LANTERN HILL. Books that are chock full of the goodness of life; most of them are set on Prince Edward Island.

Porter, Gene Stratton. A GIRL OF LIMBERLOST. FRECKLES. LADDIE. Old books that verge on being too sentimental, but their joy in the physical world and a certain magic in their story and setting place them firmly in the "best books" category for many who rediscover Porter.

Seredy, Kate. THE GOOD MASTER. THE SINGING TREE. THE CHESTRY OAK. Great stories of Hungarian families during the war. THE TENEMENT TREE. City life. These books convey a rich sense of the meaning and worth of traditions in family life.

Spyri, Johanna. HEIDI. Spyri could be called the Lucy M. Montgomery of Switzerland. Of all her many good books, HEIDI is the only one currently available in English and it deserves its place on booklists of favourites and classics. It is also surprisingly full of Christian faith. Tomi Ungerer has illustrated a beautiful edition of this which has been revised to follow the original wording more closely.

St. John, Patricia. TREASURES OF THE SNOW. TANGLEWOODS
SECRET. The children in these books are *real*—sometimes good,
sometimes horrid, and always struggling to reconcile these two inner directions. The books bring scriptural teaching solidly to bear
on the conflicts in a credible way that few explicitly "Christian" books
manage to pull off.

Twain, Mark (Samuel Clemens). TOM SAWYER. The classic boy's adventure story. Tom, half-scamp and half-hero, turns life in an American river-town into a long series of adventures.

🌺

New Favourites

Corriveau, Monique. A PERFECT DAY FOR KITES. A boy helps his
widowed, depressed father recover his creative ability and zest for
life.

Edwards, Julie. (Otherwise known as Julie Andrews, of "The Sound of
Music" fame.) THE LAST OF THE REALLY GREAT
WHANGDOODLES. MANDY. Not great writing, but wonderful
stories, the first about an imaginary country and the second about
an orphan who longs for a family.

Ellis, Sarah. NEXT-DOOR NEIGHBOURS. The neighbours were for-
eign and odd—but proved to be good friends.

Fine, Anne. FLOUR BABIES. Simon Martin and his class are assigned
the task of caring for a sack of flour for three weeks as though it were
a baby. Simon becomes quite entranced with his flour baby and
begins to think about his parents, his own potential as a parent, and
all that having a baby entails. Quite a humorous—and thoughtful—book.

Fleischman, Paul. SEED FOLKS. A very short little book set in the inner
city of Cleveland, Ohio. Each chapter is written in the voice of a

different character, all of whom help and are helped by an empty lot as it is gradually transformed into a community garden.

Hautzig, Esther. RICHES. A short and great mythic little story about an old couple who learn what true happiness and meaning are all about.

Horvath, Polly. THE TROLLS. Aunt Sally comes to babysit the children while Mother and Father go on vacation. She is an outlandish character who won't allow the kids to eat green beans and who tells wild, tall tales—sometimes hilarious, sometimes tragic—through which she communicates important bits of family history.

Konigsburg, E. L. FROM THE MIXED-UP FILES OF MRS. BASIL E. FRANKWEILER. The best of hide-and-seek in amidst the best of art. THE VIEW FROM SATURDAY. A story about friendship between children who normally wouldn't mix: what they share turns out to be more important than their differences.

Lee, Harper. TO KILL A MOCKINGBIRD. Characters and images to last a lifetime! Set in the American South, this great book teaches much about both prejudice and personhood.

L'Engle, Madeleine. MEET THE AUSTINS. One of several realistic books about the Austin family which some children love far better than L'Engle's fantasies.

Little, Jean. FROM ANNA and LISTEN TO THE SINGING. Anna struggles with poor eyesight *and* prejudice. A good sense of the need for family support in these books.

MacLachlan, Patricia. BABY. One of the finest gifts of recent fiction— for any age. Though the book would have to be read aloud to young children, it manages to defy any attempt to be categorized—by age, by type or even by genre. Ostensibly "family realism," this small volume holds a rich lode of wisdom in a simple, multi-faceted gem of a story that verges on fairy tale. See also SARAH, PLAIN AND TALL and JOURNEY.

Morpurgo, Michael. THE BUTTERFLY LION. THE KING OF THE CLOUD FOREST. THE DANCING BEAR. THE WRECK OF THE ZANZIBAR. WHEN THE WHALES CAME. KENSUKE'S KINGDOM. Wonderful stories—many with the feeling of an historical setting—*and* with integrity of character! Often they describe a unique relationship between an animal and a person.

Paperny, Myra. THE WOODEN PEOPLE. Young children of an immigrant family find relief from feeling strange and rejected—and find friends—through their own creativity.

Paterson, Katherine. THE GREAT GILLY HOPKINS. BRIDGE TO TERABITHIA. "Problem books" with real children and strong values. See also COME SING, JIMMY JO and PARK'S QUEST.

Peck, Robert Newton. ARLY. Arly Poole, like all the other citizens of Jailtown, seems caught in a downward spiral of physical and moral degradation. A preacher, Brother Smith, and a teacher, Miss Binnie Hoe, help him escape the pattern. See also A DAY NO PIGS WOULD DIE.

Sachar, Louis. HOLES. A tall tale, a fable, and an adventure all rolled into one story about Stanley Yelnats, stinky running shoes, kissing Kate Barlow (the outlaw), a camp (where all anyone does is dig holes), wild onions, poisonous lizards, and a curse. Amazingly enough, *all* the loose threads are woven neatly into the conclusion of the novel.

Schmidt, Gary D. THE SIN EATER. The Sin Eater takes pain, sorrow, and sin and changes them into grace, love and hope. Full of Christian truth and family love, it completely avoids triteness, sentimentality and "churchiness."

Spinelli, Jerry. MANIAC McGEE. Verging on fantasy, this book is the story of a orphan boy in search of a home. On his way, he helps a succession of homeless and alienated loners find companionship.

Sutcliff, Rosemary. THE LANTERN BEARERS. SUN HORSE, MOON HORSE. No list of favourites could be complete without Sutcliff. (See **Historical Fiction**.)

Voigt, Cynthia. A SOLITARY BLUE. DICEY'S SONG. Two of the Tillerman books—a series which bears the hallmark of Voigt's worth: A writer whose characters face real problems and *work* through them. Voigt does *NOT* give cheap answers—at least in these two books. See also THE CALLENDAR PAPERS and JACKAROO.

White, Ruth. BELLE PRATER'S BOY. Gypsy has lost a father, and Woodrow her cousin has lost a mother. The two of them now live side by side in a small town in Virginia in the 1950's. Though often humorous, this book deals with serious subjects: forgiving parents for desertion and suicide, and being strong enough to continue in a world with which your parents could not cope.

Adventures

French, Harry W. THE LANCE OF KANANA. A moving, powerful story of an Arabian desert boy's quest. Out of print and unavailable, but try to find it!

Hobbs, Will. FAR NORTH. A plane crash strands two boys and a Dene elder at Virginia Falls on the Neganni River at the beginning of winter. An adventure/survival story with an appreciation of Dene culture, Dene spirituality, and *cold*.

Mowat, Farley. LOST IN THE BARRENS. THE CURSE OF THE VIKING GRAVE. Two of the best of many good books by a great storyteller.

Paulsen, Gary. THE HATCHET and BRIAN'S WINTER. Two adventure stories set in the Canadian Northwoods. The first is about Brian's summer fending for himself in the wilderness with only his axe and his slowly sharpening wits. The second carries on the story—as though the fairly simplistic ending in THE HATCHET hadn't happened.

Ransome, Arthur. SWALLOWS AND AMAZONS. In the Lake District, a group of English children in love with boats begin imaginary adventures but end up experiencing real ones. The first of many excellent "Swallows and Amazons" books.

Stevenson, Robert Louis. TREASURE ISLAND. KIDNAPPED. THE BLACK ARROW. DAVID BALFOUR. A master storyteller of daring deeds, high adventure and hidden treasure—great books for boys.

Taylor, Theodore. THE CAY. An old black man and a white boy face the reality of being marooned on an island *and* with each other. After reading this book, read TIMOTHY OF THE CAY. Both a prequel *and* a sequel, this book adds nuance and depth to the story.

Some [children] like fantasies and marvels . . . and so do some adults. Some of them, like some of us, are omnivorous.

—C. S. Lewis

12

Prolific Authors for
Avid Readers

The trouble with raising a young reader is the constant chore of satisfying his or her voracious appetite for books, books, and more books—anything to *Read.* As responsible parents and teachers or aunts and uncles we nobly endeavour to bring them the meatiest literature they can swallow and digest. But just as we also need potatoes and rice to help fill our tummies, avid readers also need such books as the prolific Marguerite Henry horse stories—or even the Hardy Boys adventure stories—to keep the print rolling in front of their hungry eyes. This omnivorous stage is when the public library becomes essential. And if you deplore the lack of meat (or even variety) as your wonderful reader goes through 37 titles by one author—remember your own "potato" books. As theologian J. I. Packer himself says, "If overloaded academic and literary people never read for their own relaxation, their brains will break!" (Packer says he read his first Agatha Christie at age 7!)

Only one is listed of *many* by the same author, often involving the same characters.

Animal Stories
Farley, Walter. THE BLACK STALLION and more horse stories.
Henry, Marguerite. KING OF THE WIND and lots more horse stories based on true stories.
Lofting, Hugh. DR. DOOLITTLE. Animal fantasy.
King-Smith, Dick. BABE: THE GALLANT PIG (in England—THE SHEEP-PIG).
Kjelgaard, Jim. BIG RED and lots more dog stories.
Morey, Walt. KAVIK THE WOLF DOG and more animal stories.
Rylant, Cynthia. HENRY AND MUDGE. Illustrated by Sucie Stevenson. Comfortable adventures with Henry and his dog, Mudge. Good chapter books for the beginning reader—and lots of them!

Odd and (Often) Small Creatures
Baum, L. Frank. THE WIZARD OF OZ and many other "Oz" books.
Jansson, Tove. FINN FAMILY MOOMINTROLL. The troll family of Moomin and their adventures through many books.
Norton, Mary. THE BORROWERS. About the small folk who live under the floorboards of our houses.
Proysen, Alf. MRS. PEPPERPOT. Many titles for early readers; fun stories about a midget lady and her husband.
Sharp, Margery. MISS BIANCA. The adventures of a mouse—with sequels!

Clever Kids Conquer the World
Bibbe, John. THE MAGIC BICYCLE. The first of a whole series of "Christian Fantasy" about a boy and his marvelous—and sometimes menacing—magic bicycle.
Blyton, Enid. FIVE FALL INTO ADVENTURE—In this book and many others. Real favourites. See also her books about the SEVEN.

Korman, Gordon. I WANT TO GO HOME! A boy utterly undermines the groupy hoop-rah of his summer camp. With side-splitting humor, Korman's many books revel in a slapstick conquering of adult inanities.

Lindgren, Astrid. PIPPI LONGSTOCKING. Stories about a real tomboy that go on in book after book of wild, irrepressible antics.

Nesbit, E. THE TREASURE SEEKERS. Nesbit was a real eccentric as an adult, but (or therefore?) she knew her child audience (and many loyal adult audiences) very well!

Fitzgerald, John D. THE GREAT BRAIN. The first of a series about an ingenious rascal.

Peck, Robert Newton. SOUP. A series of books—great for boys. Adventures in the vein of all-time pranksters Huck Finn and Tom Sawyer.

Warner, Gertrude. THE BOXCAR CHILDREN. Orphans create their own life in a boxcar. This first book (of many!) is a wonderful, childlike "let's pretend." The many sequels are definitely only palatable to the avid reader.

Family Stories

Alcott, Louisa May. LITTLE WOMEN.

L'Engle, Madeleine. MEET THE AUSTINS. One of several good books involving the Austins.

McKay, Hilary. THE EXILES. This and the sequels are about a family of highly opinionated girls who love to read books.

Ransome, Arthur. SWALLOWS AND AMAZONS. One of *many* books about children on summer holidays on boats—"real" children, "real" adventure. These are fine, quiet, leisurely books that may need to be read aloud to override modern dither.

Taylor, Sidney. ALL-OF-A-KIND FAMILY. Comfortable and captivating stories of five girls (and their lone brother) in a Jewish family.

Travers, P. L. MARY POPPINS. The Banks family is taken in hand by a vain and fantastical nanny.

Comics

If you must read comics, these are the best:

Herge. THE ADVENTURES OF TINTIN. At least 20 delightful comics about Tintin, a reporter, and his sea captain friend Captain Haddock, as well as a host of minor characters. Tintin travels the world and even the moon on his adventures.

Goscinny and Uderzo. ASTERIX. There are at least 25 comics concerning Asterix, his enormous friend Obelix, and their Gaulish village surrounded by Roman camps. These comics are full of puns and plays on Latin. Really quite intellectual if you need any more justification!

Watterson, Bill. CALVIN AND HOBBES. With extraordinary vocabulary, incredible energy, and bizarre imagination, Calvin and his tiger Hobbes survive in a world of parents and babysitters. Don't try to read just one at a time; it's impossible.

Read as a child, freshly;
Read as an adult, deeply.

—Betsy Hearne

I will sing with the spirit,
I will sing with the understanding also.
—1 Corinthians 14:15b

13

Alternatives to "Young Adult" Fiction

Seasoned twelve- or thirteen-year-old readers often hit some major roadblocks in reading. For one thing, in their omnivorous appetite for books they have devoured a good share of the literature that is in the "children's" section of the library. They simply want more. Many of them also share an increasing frustration with the "problem" orientation of many books aimed at readers aged eleven to seventeen. Over and over they complain, "Too many problems!" As one young boy put it, "I read the blurb on the back cover, and if the book's about death or divorce, I won't even open it." And often the biggest "problem" young readers claim is that they want long books, and the young adult books rarely go over 150 pages.

These frustrations with young adult literature are, in the end, all part of the same problem: the young readers are growing up, and they long for books that satisfy more thoroughly, at a deeper level, and for a longer time. This age is an awkward time for them. They not only grow out of clothes, but out of books. Often, they can be so frustratingly caught in this bookish no man's land between young adult and adult literature that they stop reading or find a substitute. Boys may turn to an exclusive diet of science fiction, whether in video games or books; girls may turn to a pseudo-adult diet of romance. Parents may throw up their hands in despair.

Except for the important step of becoming a reader, no stage is as pivotal in a reader's life. Parents and teachers played a crucial role in helping the youngsters learn to read; now they often need to play the tricky role of weaning young adults from children's literature to good adult reading. The trouble is that twelve and thirteen year olds are not ready for James Joyce's ULYSSES or John Updike's RABBIT, RUN. But they are getting there. So the path into adult literature seems at times to run along a narrow ledge between the heights of complex and sophisticated literature on the one hand (ULYSSES and RABBIT, RUN) and the pits of seamy thrillers on the other (cheap sci-fi and romance). (And much of science fiction is high-quality literature, but you have to search to find it.) Here is where parents need to relax a little about some of the steps off the path (see the "Parental Guidance" section in **Helps Along the Way to Good Books for Children**). Guidance is important, but perhaps the best guidance is not what we give them to read, but what we read ourselves.

The books in this section are not all *great* books; some serve mainly as fillers for the omnivorous reader of this stage. They have all, however, proven to be helpful for this in-between stage in a young reader's life. Many of them are long. A book by Dickens doesn't zero in on a multifaceted problem of a particular phase of life; rather, it takes us through the life of David Copperfield or Nicholas Nickleby or Pip. We see the choices that make for a certain direction in the *whole* of life. We come closer to the overarching and all-inclusive Biblical pattern of Story. These are books for readers to live in, and with, and through.

Adams, Richard. WATERSHIP DOWN. THE PLAGUE DOGS. Great, long, literary masterpieces about rabbits and dogs.

Blanchet, M. Wylie. THE CURVE OF TIME. Real-life adventures of a Vancouver Island widow and her children as they cruise the fjords and islands of the inland passage. (Often available on the British Columbia Ferries and well worth your money if you live on the BC coast.)

Boyle, Kay. AVALANCHE. A spy-thriller, an alpine skiing adventure, and a love-story—all in one!

Burnford, Sheila. BEL RIA. From the author of THE INCREDIBLE JOURNEY we have yet another incredible animal survival story set in France and England during World War II.

Card, Orson Scott. ENDER'S GAME. On a space station in the future, Ender prepares a group of boys to fight a war-to-the-death with "Buggers," extra-terrestrial invaders. He is very good at what he does, but he is a pacifist at heart, which makes this an extraordinarily powerful and very unusual story (along with three good sequels). Card, a highly-regarded science fiction writer, is also a devout Mormon, and a *basic* Christian ethic comes through strongly in this story.

Chase, Mary Ellen. WINDSWEPT. A story of a New England family, full of memorable characters on the bleak and beautiful coast of Maine.

Coatsworth, Elizabeth. THE ENCHANTED. "The classic romance of the American earth." About a farmer in Maine who marries an enchanted girl.

Cooper, James Fenimore. THE DEERSLAYER. First of several Indian stories. Mark Twain pokes fun at the blade-and-twig tracking techniques of Cooper's heroes, but, phony though they may be, these books are great adventure stories.

Costain, Thomas B. THE BLACK ROSE, THE SILVER CHALICE (his best) and other titles. Prolific writer of historical fiction. Second rate, but good "fillers."

Craven, Margaret. I HEARD THE OWL CALL MY NAME. A sad but beautiful story of a young priest dying in a native village on Canada's west coast.

Cronin, A. J. THE CITADEL. A young doctor discovers the difference between the goals of earning money and helping people.

Dickens, Charles. A TALE OF TWO CITIES and DAVID COPPERFIELD. And many more great nineteenth-century novels.

Doyle, Sir Arthur Conan. THE HOUND OF THE BASKERVILLES. A Sherlock Holmes thriller by the author of all the other classic Sherlock Holmes stories.

Dumas, Alexandre. THE COUNT OF MONTE CHRISTO. A fully satisfying, long book of French romance and adventure.

Freedman, Nancy and Benedict. MRS. MIKE. A story of the eastern bride of an RCMP (Royal Canadian Mounted Police) in the Canadian North—blend of heart-throb romance and tragic realism. A true story.

Goudge, Elizabeth. THE DEAN'S WATCH. A CITY OF BELLS. And many others. Satisfying stories of real (though fictional) people in England. A favourite—THE SCENT OF WATER. Also, a trilogy which reveals both the pain and the glory that permeate life in a family: THE BIRD IN THE TREE. PILGRIM'S INN (or THE HERB OF GRACE). THE HEART OF THE FAMILY.

Graham, Robin Lee. DOVE. A boy describes sailing around the world—for real! Hunt for the sequel, too—HOME IS THE HUNTER.

Henderson, Zenna. THE PEOPLE. PILGRIMAGE. Powerful, very *human* science fiction about a community of *very* gifted, caring people who have to hide their gifts and their origin. Some wonderful insights in these books about faith in action. Also, HOLDING WONDER.

Herbert, Frank. DUNE. One of *the* great works of science fiction. Just as Paul (son of Duke Atreides, ruler of a planet) is entering manhood, his family is forced to move from their lush, tropical planet to a harsh, desert planet (hence the title). And as if that weren't enough disruption, the natives (and even Paul himself) begin to notice that he seems to fulfil the ancient prophesies of a messiah come to free the people and restore the land. (Beware: there *are* sequels, but the quality is halved each book.)

Herriot, James. ALL THINGS BRIGHT AND BEAUTIFUL. —Etc. Adventures and traumas of an animal doctor in England—*and* his patients—and their owners!

Heyerdahl, Thor. KON-TIKI. A true adventure on the seas. Heyerdahl describes his attempt to re-enact a major primitive migration in the South Pacific.

Innes, Hammond. CAMPBELL'S KINGDOM—and many others. Called "a master of high adventure" and "a whale of a writer," Innes is a captivating and prolific storyteller.

L'Amour, Louis. THE CHEROKEE TRAIL. Get started on L'Amour and you'll have at least a year's worth of fine, 'filler,' escape literature ahead of you—cowboys and Indians at their best. This one has a woman hero!

Lewis, C. S. OUT OF THE SILENT PLANET. PERELANDRA. THAT HIDEOUS STRENGTH. His excellent space trilogy.

MacDonald, George. (Phelps, Michael—reteller) THE BARONET'S SONG. THE SHEPHERD'S CASTLE. And many more re-tellings of wonderful stories by George MacDonald, of whom C. S. Lewis said, "[he] baptized my imagination."

Marshall, Catherine. CHRISTY. JULIE. Two books, set in the Appalachian mountians, about strong young women who make hard choices.

McPhee, John. COMING INTO THE COUNTRY. ENCOUNTERS WITH THE ARCH-DRUID. THE DELTOID PUMPKIN SEED. CURVE OF BINDING ENERGY. And others. Superbly-written journalistic accounts of everything from rafting the Grand Canyon to building atomic bombs.

Nordhoff, Charles and James Norman Hall. MUTINY ON THE BOUNTY. MEN AGAINST THE SEA. PITCAIRN'S ISLAND. The adventures and misfortunes of some eighteenth century British sailors who arrive at a South Sea paradise and then decide to mutiny rather than leave it—as well as the adventures of the officers who were thrown off the boat by their rebellious crew.

O'Brian, Patrick. MASTER AND COMMANDER. The first of a series of historical sea adventure novels. The characters are *real* and therefore sometimes rather unsavoury, but they mature as the books go on and thereby become windows on the complexity of human character. Full of lore from the days of the old sailing ships.

Orezy, Baronness. THE SCARLET PIMPERNEL. A suspenseful story of the French Revolution.

Orwell, George. 1984. Orwell's classic continues to ring true long past its apparent "expiry date." As long as there are governments willing to misuse words in order to subdue and control the masses, and as long as there is omnipresent electronic media, this book will remain relevant.

Paton, Alan. CRY THE BELOVED COUNTRY. TOO LATE THE PHALAROPE. Beautiful, sad stories of apartheid and prejudice in South Africa.

Peters, Ellis. (Edith Pargeter) Any of the BROTHER CADFAEL books, beginning with A MORBID TASTE FOR BONES. A find for avid readers: medieval mysteries with just enough theology and history to make you *know* you're settling in for a good, worthwhile read. (Good to read in order.)

Potok, Chaim. MY NAME IS ASHER LEV. THE PROMISE. THE CHOSEN. DAVITA'S HARP. Excellent novels about Hasidic Jews in America.

Richter, Conrad. THE TREES. THE FIELDS. THE TOWNS. Change in the landscape brings changes in people during the settlement of North America.

Sayers, Dorothy L. THE NINE TAILORS. MURDER MUST ADVER-TISE. And many others. Mystery novels full of humor, intelligence, and suspense.

Shute, Nevil. A TOWN LIKE ALICE. THE PIED PIPER. TRUSTEE FROM THE TOOLROOM. MOST SECRET. And others! Wonderful books on the resilience and persistence of the human spirit by a fine storyteller.

Twain, Mark (Samuel Clemens). THE ADVENTURES OF HUCKLEBERRY FINN. Huckleberry Finn and the runaway slave Jim get away from it all and float down the Mississippi River. Superficially a comic continuation of the adventures of Tom Sawyer and Huckleberry Finn, this book moves far beyond boyish antics to deep beauty and meaning.

White, T. H. THE ONCE AND FUTURE KING. Hilarious retelling of the Arthurian story.

These next two books are specifically geared to the teenage audience, *and (but?!) are very good.*

Le Guin, Ursula K. VERY FAR AWAY FROM ANYWHERE ELSE. Two teenagers reject intensifying their own relationship and opt instead for a relationship that will help them with their goals for the future in education and vocation.

Randle, Kristen D. BREAKING RANK. Cathy, a *nice* girl, tutors Baby, a member of an all-male, black-clothed gang. Both they and the reader struggle in an adolescent journey through stereotypes of friendship, family and religion to trust.

I am almost inclined to set it up as a canon that a children's story which is enjoyed only by children is a bad children's story. The good ones last . . . the neat sorting-out of books into age-groups, so dear to publishers, has only a very sketchy relation with the habits of any real readers. Those of us who are blamed when old for reading childish books were blamed when children for reading books too old for us. No reader worth his salt trots along in obedience to a time-table.

—C.S. Lewis

Perhaps it is only in childhood that books have any deep influence on our lives . . . . But in childhood all books are books of divination, telling us about the future, and like the fortune teller who sees a long journey in the cards or death by water they influence the future.

—Grahame Greene

A bookseller . . . is the link between mind and mind, the feeder of the hungry, very often the binder-up of wounds. There he sits, your bookseller, surrounded by a thousand minds all done up neatly in cardboard cases; beautiful minds, courageous minds, strong minds, wise minds, all sorts and conditions. And there come into him other minds, hungry for beauty, for knowledge, for truth, for love, and to the best of his ability he satisfies them all. . . . Yes. . . . It's a great vocation.

—Elizabeth Goudge

14

Helps Along the Way to Good Books for Children

✿

Family Reading

A child, a book, and a lap—that is the birthplace of the love of books, every bit as much as the Fertile Crescent was the birthplace of human civilization. And at the risk of sounding hyperbolic, that combination probably provides the greatest nurture for human culture in our time. For by hearing words in their rich complexity we learn the art of communicating our thoughts—our hopes and concerns and love—first to our own family and then to the community of the human family. In books we learn to understand the thinking, hopes and fears of people other than ourselves, and in reading them together we dip into the deep, shared well of human experience and understanding.

Reading aloud together as a family, like most good things in life, takes a fair amount of plain old commitment. Establishing the habit may take hard work and some creativity, especially in timing, but once the habit of reading aloud is a firm part of the family structure, it will usually stick—even in the teenage years—or even after the kids leave home.

Here are ten good reasons to take the time and trouble to establish the habit of a family time for reading. Such reading:

1. Builds in an opportunity for physical closeness. Reading one book together automatically involves a natural and unselfconscious intimacy. Pajamas, a covered mattress on the floor, and a comforter to spread over all the laps—wrap parents and children in a cocoon of coziness caught best by the all-encompassing German word *Gemütlichkeit* (perhaps best translated, "hearts and minds united in joy and affection").

2. Provides an introduction to good literature. The selection of quality books to justify all the reading aloud time automatically insures an introduction to *good books*—often of the sort that children would not choose to read on their own.

3. Creates occasions for the discussion of literary and moral virtues. Often questions and issues that we would like to talk over with our children come up easily and naturally in the context of reading aloud. A good book deals honestly and richly with life, and therefore, as in real life, what to do is not always clear, and what happens is hard to take or seems unjust. "Why oh why . . . ?" both we and our children ask. Or "How?" The whys and hows of books and life quickly get down to questions of psychology, morality, and theology.

Such talks will also sharpen our children's literary understanding. Greatness of writing is intrinsically tied to greatness of thought. The hows and whys of imagery, character portrayal and plot development give depth and richness to the questions and issues.

In the discussions which will definitely result from reading aloud, we need as parents—or aunts, uncles, grandparents, friends—to avoid jumping into the issues with all four feet. We need to make sure the talking stays a conversation rather than a lecture. Letting a child lead the discussion will mean that the questions appropriate for his or her stage of thinking will be dealt with instead of being lost in a morass of adult conundrums.

4. Increases skill in reading. Children might possibly learn to read early as they look over their parent's shoulder, but they become readers for life far more through listening. Early readers are often not *Readers*.

5. Builds an appreciation for words. Reading aloud is as close as many will get to an oral tradition in which storytellers chose words and word patterns with a care and cadence that built them into the oral "genetic code" of human thought.

6. Spans age differences. A worthy "chapter book"—such as CHARLOTTE'S WEB, the Narnia Books, or THE WIND IN THE WILLOWS—can be listened to at a much younger age than it can be read on one's own. And no one should ever be too old to savour and relish a good children's book.

7. Provides reference points for family allusions. Phrases, characters, descriptions, heard and "lived" by the whole family, become short cuts for saying a lot with a little. Affirming with a groan that bad things happen ". . .even in Australia" (from Judith Viorst's ALEXANDER AND THE TERRIBLE, HORRIBLE, NO-GOOD, VERY BAD DAY) has lightened the misery of many a mishap. "Don't be so cocky and self-congratulating and confident that you can conquer all, because in the long run it is gentleness and kindness and thinking of others more than yourself that will accomplish good and lasting relationships" can all be said in "don't be a Steerforth"(a notorious character from Charles Dickens' DAVID COPPERFIELD).

8. Substitutes for TV. Weaning children from TV (of course it's better if they never get addicted to it in the first place) can demand a high level of planned activity. Reading is a low energy, easily planned alternative that has an invaluable side effect. Listening to stories activates the imagination. But TV, on the other hand, gives all *except the imagination* to the viewer: voice, sound, facial features and expressions, setting, clothes, interpretation—there is nothing left to imagine. Gone, too, is any possibility for an imaginative immersion of oneself in a character and the resultant therapeutic exploration in role-playing thought that brings maturity and understanding.

9. Provides a Survival Kit for family trips. Hours of miles are endlessly and happily whiled away if books are part of the baggage. We remember reading through an Ursula K. Le Guin novel on an 8-hour trip. We were all so eager to finish that we stopped a hundred yards from our destination to finish the book before the trip ended. And if a trip can be tied in with books—Roman Britain with Rosemary Sutcliff, North American midwest prairies with Wilder's Little House books—the places we visit will have a liveliness of historical presence that will, with time, mature into a mythic "Remembrance of Trips Past."

10. Puts good stuff in the Pot. Books read aloud remain a solid mental and emotional heritage for children (as well as for their parents). As Jane Yolen puts it:

> Take one small child and throw into the bubbling pot of its mind all that it sees and hears: TV, superheroes and superstars, cartoons, mother's and father's opinions, the teacher's assertions, the misrepresentations of its peers. What comes out is a semi-coherent mythology that the child carries into adulthood. I believe that a child—and an adult—needs a mythology.

Deciding to start a brand new family tradition such as reading aloud can seem like yet one more big, daunting "ought" to worry about. Here are five suggestions to help make sure that your Family Reading actually *happens.*

1. 100% Attendance: As much as possible, everyone should be included—especially both parents. Their presence says to the children: this time together with each other and books is important. Often younger children don't have the attention span for even a "young" chapter book of the sort that would still be enjoyable by a whole family. In that case, try to time the reading after the young ones have been put to bed. (They get their own bedtime story, of course!) The incentive to stay up just a little longer to take part in this family ritual will do wonders for their attention span as they get older.

2. Regular Time: Building reading into the family schedule will not only ensure that it happens, but may well help deflect some of the scattered, unfocussed multi-directional busy-ness that saps many families of their communal core. (The same attention needs to be spent on eating meals together, but that's another subject.) As children get older, reading can be a study break. (See Number 5!)

3. Whole Books: Avoid short stories or loosely-tied episodes. Suspense holds successive evenings securely together. When "what happens next?" is in everyone's mind all day, there will be no problem in getting together for the evening's reading.

4. No Reading Ahead: Children *or parents!* The book may be a re-read for some or all of the listeners—but let it have its own life in your life together as a family by allowing it to unfold in your read-aloud time.

5. Popcorn: Make the reading time a celebration with heaping bowls of popcorn! Especially as children get older, the smell of popcorn—and maybe even the promise of hot chocolate with marshmallows—will do all the luring that's needed.

And finally, to give you a good start, here are some tried and true books for reading aloud:

7-111 Books: For those from age 7 (or even as young as 4) to over 100— perfect for the middle-aged, multi-aged family.

Alexander, Lloyd. The PRYDAIN Chronicles.

Atwater, Richard and Florence. MR. POPPER'S PENGUINS.

Burnett, Frances Hodgson. THE SECRET GARDEN. THE LITTLE PRINCESS. THE LOST PRINCE.

Burnford, Sheila. THE INCREDIBLE JOURNEY.

French, Harry. THE LANCE OF KANANA.

Grahame, Kenneth. THE WIND IN THE WILLOWS.

Henry, Marguerite. KING OF THE WIND.

Kendall, Carol. THE GAMMAGE CUP.

Lewis, C. S. THE LION, THE WITCH AND THE WARDROBE (all the Narnia books).

MacDonald, George. SIR GIBBIE. (Available in a non-dialect edition edited by Elizabeth Yates) THE PRINCESS AND THE GOBLIN.

Montgomery, Lucy M. ANNE OF GREEN GABLES.

O'Dell, Scott. ISLAND OF THE BLUE DOLPHINS.

Roberts, Sir Charles G. D. RED FOX.

Salten, Felix. BAMBI (not the Disney version!).

Spyri, Johanna. HEIDI.

Sutcliff, Rosemary. WARRIOR SCARLET. SUN HORSE, MOON HORSE. THE EAGLE OF THE NINTH. THE SHIELD RING. DAWN WIND. THE SHINING COMPANY. THE LANTERN BEARERS.

Tolkien, J. R. R. THE HOBBIT. THE LORD OF THE RINGS.

White, E. B. CHARLOTTE'S WEB.

White, T. H. MISTRESS MASHAM'S REPOSE.

Wilder, Laura Ingalls. LITTLE HOUSE IN THE BIG WOODS. And all the rest of the Little House books.

For the "older" family, for "empty-nesters" and for good friends.

Adams, Richard. WATERSHIP DOWN. THE PLAGUE DOGS. SHARDIK.

Berry, Wendell. FIDELITY.

Bunyan, John. PILGRIM'S PROGRESS.

Chesterton, G. K. THE MAN WHO WAS THURSDAY.

Dickens, Charles. A TALE OF TWO CITIES. DAVID COPPERFIELD. GREAT EXPECTATIONS.

Lewis, C. S. OUT OF THE SILENT PLANET. PERELANDRA. THAT HIDEOUS STRENGTH. SCREWTAPE LETTERS.

MacDonald, George. THE BARONET'S SONG. THE SHEPHERD'S CASTLE. And lots more re-tellings of the MacDonald novels by Michael Phillips.

Peters, Ellis (Edith Pargeter) "BROTHER CADFAEL" books. In order! Also THE "HEAVEN TREE" TRILOGY.

Sayers, Dorothy L. THE NINE TAILORS. And many other Peter Whimsey books.

Shute, Nevil. TRUSTEE FROM THE TOOLROOM. THE PIED PIPER.

Sutcliff, Rosemary. SWORD AT SUNSET.

Tolkien, J. R. R. THE LORD OF THE RINGS.

The Family Library

A family library is a literary legacy for your children, your grandchildren, your great grandchildren and yet more generations in the future. My grandchildren will inherit books I've inherited from my grandmother. That's five generations. And many a family that is not composed of immigrants as recent as mine could claim an even longer library legacy.

But good books cost money—lots of it. Hardback books especially seem almost a profligate luxury. Two considerations help put the matter in perspective:

1) A book costs the same (about $25) as a good meal with coffee and dessert in an average restaurant.

2) To build a good family library costs the equivalent of three restaurant meals per child per year. *And* careful hunts at second hand bookstores may well get them at fast food prices—or lower. Maybe a third consideration should be added—a good quality, hardbound book is a lasting investment in the life and mind of a child.

If you buy one good hardback book per year for each child for Christmas, for a birthday present, and for one other special occasion (Easter, Summer vacation, etc.), then in ten years the child will have a library of thirty-three fine hardback volumes that he or she will very promptly claim (to your chagrin) when setting up a home. Here is a list of suggestions for those three books a year per child, from birth to ten years of age. For more details, check annotated listings.

Birthday Books

Birth GOODNIGHT MOON. Margaret Wise Brown.
1 I WENT WALKING. Julie Vivas.
2 WHERE THE WILD THINGS ARE. Maurice Sendak.
3 JOHNNY CROW'S GARDEN. L. Leslie Brooke.
4 THE LITTLE HOUSE or MIKE MULLIGAN AND HIS STEAM SHOVEL. Virginia Lee Burton.
5 TIME OF WONDER. Robert McCloskey.
6 WHEN WE WERE VERY YOUNG or NOW WE ARE SIX. A. A. Milne.
7 STONE FOX. John Gardiner.
8 THE SECRET GARDEN. Frances Hodgson Burnett. Or HOMER PRICE. Robert McCloskey.
9 KING OF THE WIND. Marguerite Henry.
10 THE ARABIAN NIGHTS.

Christmas Books

Birth THE FRIENDLY BEASTS. Illustrated by Sarah Chamberlain.
1 READ-ALOUD BIBLE STORIES. Edited by Ella K. Lindvall.
2 STORIES JESUS TOLD. Nick Butterworth and Mick Inkpen.
3 TO EVERY THING THERE IS A SEASON. Leo and Diane Dillon.
4 BIBLE STORIES FOR CHILDREN (Macmillan).
5 THE HOBBIT. J. R. R. Tolkien.
6 THE LION, THE WITCH AND THE WARDROBE. C. S. Lewis. (Get deluxe edition published by Harper Collins in 1997, or the whole set—but in hardback.)
7 THE PRINCESS AND THE GOBLIN. George MacDonald.

8   PILGRIM'S PROGRESS. John Bunyan. (See edition by Gary Schmidt.)
9   SOUNDER. William Armstrong.
10   THE LORD OF THE RINGS (trilogy). J. R. R. Tolkien.

Special Occasions

Birth MY VERY FIRST MOTHER GOOSE or HERE COMES MOTHER GOOSE. Edited by Iona Opie and illustrated by Rosemary Wells.
1   THE CIRCLE OF DAYS. Reeve Lindbergh. Illustrated by Cathie Felstead.
2   NUTSHELL LIBRARY. Maurice Sendak.
3   THE TALE OF PETER RABBIT. Beatrix Potter.
4   TALKING LIKE THE RAIN. Edited by X. J. and Dorothy Kennedy. Illustrated by Jane Dyer.
5   LITTLE HOUSE IN THE BIG WOODS. Laura Ingalls Wilder.
6   TALES FROM GRIMM. Edited by Wanda Gag.
7   THE WIND IN THE WILLOWS. Kenneth Grahame.
8   BOOK OF GREEK MYTHS. Ingri and Edgar Parin D'Aulaire.
9   WARRIOR SCARLET or THE EAGLE OF THE NINTH. Rosemary Sutcliff.
10   WATERSHIP DOWN. Richard Adams.

Help and Inspiration for Parents

Here is a list of books that very roughly follows the same underlying patterns as the suggested library acquisition choices. These books add depth of meaning and rich insight to our enjoyment of books with our children—as well as to their books.

Pre-Natal   BABIES NEED BOOKS. Dorothy Butler.
1   THE OXFORD DICTIONARY OF NURSERY RHYMES. Iona and Peter Opie.
2   HONEY FOR A CHILD'S HEART. Gladys Hunt.
3   THE PLUG-IN DRUG. Marie Winn.
4   "On Fairy Stories," in THE TOLKIEN READER. J. R. R. Tolkien.
5   FIVE TO EIGHT. Dorothy Butler.

Parental Guidance Suggested

The issue that always lurks behind the label "PG" is censorship: Are there some books, magazines, and videos to which we should say a flat "No"?

To begin with, let's agree that there are books, magazines and videos which not only children, but no adult should see or read either (ironically, they are usually found in a section labeled "adult"). But what about all the other stuff we'd rather our kids not read, either because it's shallow and trivial, or because "they're not old enough yet"? How should we say "No"? Or should we say "No" at all?

As Flannery O'Connor, the great southern Catholic Christian writer says of her audience, "There are many Catholic [we could just as well broaden this to Christian parent] readers who open up a novel and, discovering the presence of an arm or a leg, piously close the book." And we could add other "finds" than arms or legs that close books equally fast. J. K. Rowling's HARRY POTTER books are closed by the presence of witches and wizards (see "The Potter Problem" below); AWAKE AND DREAMING by Kit Pearson is closed for mentioning a girl with two mommies; and BRIDGE TO TERABITHIA and THE GREAT GILLY HOPKINS by Katherine Paterson are closed due to one or two "damn"s and "hell"s. Even such classics as The Narnia Books and THE SECRET GARDEN have been closed because of the presence of "magic."

As Christian parents or friends of children we do have much to worry about in a culture so confused that it can protest even using words like "good" and "bad" to describe choices in behaviour. Many today try to claim that all choices are "good," simply because they are individual and personal. Today the question is often not (as it has been for centuries)

"Is it true?" or "Is it right?", referring to some larger framework of absolutes, but "Is it true *for me*?" or "Is it moral *for me*?" And so, as a part of this new "for Me" morality, all possibilities are opened to individual choice—from tidied-up biblical stories (which omit many of the earthy realities in the full biblical narrative of flesh and blood humanity) to videos of extreme violence and sexual perversion. Sometimes, it seems, we do have to "Just say 'No.'"

At this point, let us back up a bit and see what happens when we say "No," especially when we say it through an overt censoring of our children's reading. The first and most obvious result of our saying, "No, you may not read that book" (and often we would need to add ". . . that you are reading" because they are already well into it) is that we clearly show a lack of trust in our children's own ability to make good choices. And that lack of trust is certainly not a way to build up in the child a pride in personal trustworthiness and a consequent eagerness to show that trustworthiness by making responsible choices. By saying a flat "No," we have in effect killed trust.

And in killing trust between ourselves and our children, we also show a lack of trust in ourselves and in our rearing of the children to be able to make responsible decisions. By the time such "censorship or guidance" situations arise, we should be able to respond to "bad books" by saying to ourselves, "I have, to the best of my ability, brought up these children in the way they should go, so why should I fear their reading this book?"

Such a response clarifies another unfortunate result of saying "No": our laying down the law cuts off opportunities for the thoughtful discussion that could result from a more rational response of asking, "Why?" That discussion might well end in our children making "No" decisions for themselves after having thought the issues over with us in a level-headed, heart-to-heart talk. Such interaction builds trust instead of killing it through a sort of intellectual violence. And such conversations mature not only our children's ability to think, but also their ability to articulate their faith and the way it shapes their lives.

One of the more devious results of killing trust and cutting off the possibility for discussion (through our saying an unequivocal "No") is that we thereby tell our child not only that we don't trust them and that discussion of our fiat is not allowable, but we also implicitly tell them that we assume their reason for reading the book is precisely because of the sex or bad words or occult content. We assume the worst. They, on the other hand, are more likely to be reading the book just because it has an exciting, fast-paced plot—or even because they are reassured by a strong sense of right and wrong that undergirds its structure, characters, and theme. Again, by simply saying "No" we have undermined trust.

And finally, saying an outright "No" ultimately says to our children that Christian truths and patterns of life are not able to hold their own against the facts of our contemporary culture. Discussion, on the other hand, rather than a straight "No" says that the "Yes" of Christian understanding is greater than the "Yes" of popular culture. Saying "No" is often a stance of fear. It teaches protective isolationism rather than healthy, and ultimately redemptive, interaction with our culture. Answering "Why? —or as scripture puts it, "be[ing] prepared to give the reason to everyone who asks you to give an answer for the hope that you have" (1 Peter 3:15) is harder, but in the end it is much stronger than saying "No."

In the long run, saying "No" should not in any case be a one-time, flash-hot response to a particular "bad book." It should instead be a process that starts at birth. The key to saying "No" is to start early in saying "Yes" to good books. The Family Reading Time is when a canon of good literature can be filed away in children's hearts and minds. And in order to create a climate for open, trusting discussion, our Reading Time should include Katherine Paterson's books, Pearson's AWAKE AND DREAMING, even the Harry Potters. These books not only raise problems that need to be openly displayed before they can be openly discussed, but they need to be discussed in the context of a Christian home or school that has provided good reading, good thinking and a good strong moral substratum that will help the children learn the huge and very important difference between books which wrestle with the problem of human evil, and books which affirm and encourage that evil.

Unfortunately many books which raise no problems at all are nevertheless totally lacking a solid moral framework. They may be unobjectionable and seem true to life on the surface—they may even be "Christian" books, but they fail to reflect the ambivalence and complexity of life that is reflected in Scripture (think of the Psalms) and in the richest products of our culture (think of Shakespeare or Dostoevsky).

Flannery O'Connor has some wise words to say to readers who close their books when they discover something objectionable:

Many . . . readers are over-conscious of what they consider to be obscenity in modern fiction for the very simple reason that in reading a book, they have nothing else to look for. They are not equipped to find anything else. They are totally unconscious of the design, the intention, the meaning, or even the truth of what they have in hand. They don't see the book in a perspective that would reduce every part of it to its proper place in the whole.

We need to see, and we need to help our children see, books in this broader perspective that includes the whole pattern and thrust of a book. We need to be readers whose moral and literary tastes have been formed by a good reading (hopefully, much of it aloud, in the family) of good literature—the classic fairy tales of Cinderlads and lassies(ellas), the Tolkien and Lewis fantasies, the Arthur Ransome family adventures, and Rosemary Sutcliff's early Britain novels. Then we and our children will be able to identify the problems that are deeply ingrained both in the overarching culture—and in our Christian sub-culture. We need to have the courage—and the faith in God, the great storyteller—to be able to use books, whether good or "bad," as ways of filling the rooms of our minds with the "rare treasures" that come from wisdom, understanding and knowledge (Proverbs 24:3-4).

Does all this mean that we never say "No"? No. But it does mean that we need to be very cautious about what we say "No" to, and that we need to say that "No" in a conversation that is honest and open, that is characterized by mutual trust and that is based on our own careful reading of the book we are rejecting (all too often our rejections are based on fearful reactions to rumours about books we have not read). And above all, we need to remember that ultimately our "Yes"es are far more powerful that our "No"s.

THE POTTER PROBLEM

This is a good place to face the recent dilemma of many Christian parents: What do we do about the HARRY POTTER books? Concerned parents would do well to read some of the excellent thinking that has been done on both sides (see **References**). These books are a prime example of the wisdom of Flannery O' Connor's plea for perspective. They are often read only in terms of their setting in a school of witchcraft. That very popular setting, however, hooks young and old into hearing two strong messages that come through over and over. First of all, those in authority (in this case the teachers of Hogwarts Academy and the leaders of the Ministry of Magic) are not always *de facto* good and trustworthy. Secondly, we have to do what is right even if it means rejection by peers.

That J. K. Rowling couches these important truths in between classes in Double Divination and spells cast by the impetuous Weasley twins shouldn't blind us to her solid teaching on right and wrong. We all share some of the devious ways in which these students and teachers of witchcraft warp the virtues of life. The stories are far more about "life" than they are about "witchcraft."

If we reject the HARRY POTTER books out of hand on the grounds of occultism, we deny our children exposure to the insights into good and evil that light up their pages. In reading them from a rigid position of rejection, we also implicitly teach our children a rigidity of response to knowledge. One day they will discover that truth in our fallen world is always a mixed bag. They will need to have learned lessons of wise discernment rather than closed-minded denial. To say "No" does not allow this wiser sifting through the complex mix of truth and falsehood, right and wrong, good and evil. And we lose a chance to prepare children for making the often muddy decisions of life when we are no longer there to say "Yes" or "No" for them.

❧

Helpful Books and Articles

Buechner, Frederick. THE ALPHABET OF GRACE. A book that encourages us to accept the truth that grace is creating *story* from the cacophony of our daily lives.

Butler, Dorothy. BABIES NEED BOOKS. FIVE TO EIGHT. Two books full of wisdom on bringing books into the lives of our children.

Chesterton, G. K. "The Ethics of Elfland," in ORTHODOXY. (See Tolkien, below.) Excellent discussion of the "magic" of fairy tales as an apologetic for God.

Druitt, Ann and Christine Fynes-Clinton and Marije Rowling. ALL YEAR ROUND. Sometimes when we read children's books it seems like lives *were* full of celebrations and traditions (more than ours are now). This book has crafts and ideas for beginning again to celebrate saints' days, holy days, and the seasons. It is very homey and chatty in style, with many ideas for using natural objects. (Don't feel obligated to do every idea in the book!) There are no "Church Year" type books in our booklist except for some Christmas books. Perhaps this book and OFFERING THE GOSPEL TO CHILDREN (see Pritchard, below) will fill that gap (as well as reading books about families with religious traditions, such as ALL-OF-A-KIND FAMILY with its detailed, loving description of Jewish holy days).

Duff, Annis. BEQUEST OF WINGS: A FAMILY'S PLEASURE WITH BOOKS. LONGER FLIGHT: A FAMILY GROWS UP WITH BOOKS. These are dated and daunting (and yet extremely inspiring and enjoyable) books about a family incorporating books (and music and art) into their daily lives, making them much richer in the process.

Egoff, Sheila. THE REPUBLIC OF CHILDHOOD: A CRITICAL GUIDE TO CANADIAN CHILDREN'S LITERATURE IN ENGLISH. A terrific resource book for finding books and for finding out how to evaluate books. Egoff taught Children's Literature at University of British Columbia for years and could well be called the Mother of Children's Literature in Canada. The book is now in its third edition with colleague Judith Saltman as co-writer: THE NEW REPUBLIC OF CHILDHOOD.

_____. Ed. ONLY CONNECT. Very helpful articles on children's literature.

_____. THURSDAY'S CHILD: TRENDS AND PATTERNS IN CONTEMPORARY CHILDREN'S LITERATURE

_____. WORLDS WITHIN: CHILDREN'S FANTASY FROM THE MIDDLE AGES TO TODAY. Excellent overview of fantasy literature by one who has kept a discerning "finger" on the pulse of fantasy for a number of years.

Frye, Northrop. THE EDUCATED IMAGINATION. A fine, brief introduction to the essential elements of story and image. THE GREAT CODE: THE BIBLE AND LITERATURE. His study of the Biblical pattern for Story.

Hazard, Paul. BOOKS, CHILDREN AND MEN. An out-of-date, politically-incorrect title for a fine old classic on the importance of books for children.

Hunt, Gladys. HONEY FOR A CHILD'S HEART. Third edition. Reading in the Christian home. Excellent wisdom from one who was both a teacher and a mother.

Kilpatrick, William and Gregory and Suzanne M. Wolfe. BOOKS THAT BUILD CHARACTER: A GUIDE TO TEACHING YOUR CHILD MORAL VALUES THROUGH STORIES. Includes lengthy descriptions of over 300 books, as well as discussions on how books can help children tell right from wrong.

Lewis, C. S. "On Three Ways of Writing for Children," in OF OTHER WORLDS. A good article to keep in mind when evaluating books that seemed to be geared toward a market demand.

Lindskoog, Kathryn and Ranelda Hunsicker. HOW TO GROW A YOUNG READER. Contains some good evaluative discussions of recent children's books.

Livingston, Myra Cohen. THE CHILD AS POET: MYTH OR REAL-ITY. This book is not about reading but about writing poetry. But it is, at the same time, an exceptionally wise and helpful introduction to poetry and to ways of helping children appreciate good poetry.

Opie, Iona and Peter. THE CLASSIC FAIRY TALES. Excellent basic collection of and introduction to fairy tales.

Owens, Virginia Stem. A FEAST OF FAMILIES. Good writing on the meaning of family.

Paterson, Katherine. GATES OF EXCELLENCE. THE SPYING HEART. Two collections of articles, reviews, and speeches which come back again and again to questions of the relationship of Christians—and of all human beings—to realistic fiction, fantasy, and fairy tales. WHO AM I? Written for 8-12 year olds to help them understand their relationship to God and to the basics of Christian belief. See also the Leader's Guide for WHO AM I?, written by Elizabeth Stickney.

Postman, Neil. THE DISAPPEARANCE OF CHILDHOOD. Very readable, very insightful book on 1) the historical connection between the rise of books and childhood, and 2) the threat to childhood as we know it posed by television, computer games, radio, and other electronic media.

Pritchard, Gretchen Wolff. OFFERING THE GOSPEL TO CHILDREN. Geared toward Christian educators in liturgical churches, this book is an eye opener to how much deeper and wider we can go in offering the Gospel to children.

Tolkien, J. R. R. "On Fairy Stories," in THE TOLKIEN READER. This essay and the Chesterton essay above are classic defenses of fairy tales and fantasy as beginning points for a pre-Christian apologetic.

Trelease, Jim. THE NEW READ-ALOUD HANDBOOK. Whys and hows for reading aloud.

Wilson, Elizabeth. BOOKS CHILDREN LOVE. Good recommendations, well-annotated, and cross-referenced for informational nonfiction as well as fiction. Organized by subject.

Winn, Marie. THE PLUG-IN DRUG: TELEVISION, CHILDREN, AND THE FAMILY. An easily readable, potentially life-changing book on the effects of TV on children and families. Another more technical book on the effects of TV is FOUR ARGUMENTS FOR THE ELIMINATION OF TELEVISION by Jerry Mander.

❦

Magazines

THE HORNBOOK. Reviews and articles on literature for children. Address: 56 Roland St., Suite 200, Boston MA 02129. Tel: (800) 325-1170. Internet: *www.hbook.com*

RIVERBANK REVIEW. A review magazine of books for young readers published with the School of Education at the University of St. Thomas. Selective and careful reviews, excellent and informative articles and interviews, a thoughtful editorial, an author profile, a detachable bookmark of 10 great books on a selected topic and a final, wonderful column rescuing some worthy book from oblivion— all characteristics of an ideal source for parents and teachers alike who want to know about children's books. Very highly recommended with several sighs of relief that there finally is such a magazine! Address: University of St. Thomas, 2115 Summit Avenue, CHC-131, St. Paul MN 55105. Tel: (651) 962-5372. Internet: *www.riverbankreview.com*

❦

Sources of Good Books

CHINABERRY—2780 Via Orange Way, Suite B, Spring Valley CA 91978. Tel: (800) 776-2242. A book and craft catalogue that is excellent except for its tendency towards "political correctness." Be careful, the ads are as tempting as those in L. L. Bean and garden catalogues! Internet: *www.chinaberry.com*

POWELL'S BOOKS—If you ever go though Portland, Oregon, hunt up the main Powell's store. It is a huge converted warehouse with rooms devoted to different subjects—a big enough children's literature section to get lost in, with second-hand and new books shelved together. They supply maps of the store at the entrances! Look for similar bookstores in your area. Internet: *www.powells.com*

BOOKSTORE—Your LOCAL bookseller will be happy to order books for you.

PUBLIC LIBRARY—Many branch libraries have a sales table. But main libraries often have *huge* yearly sales where you can get *cheap,* high quality books. Call to find the date.

INTERNET—The best source for specific, out-of-print books. Try *www.bookfinder.com,* among others.

A book is a cooperative venture. The writer can write a story down, but the book will never be complete until a reader of whatever age takes that book and brings to it his own story.
—Katherine Paterson

Literary experience heals the wound, without undermining the privilege, of individuality . . . in reading great literature I become a thousand men and yet remain myself. Like the night sky in the Greek poem, I see with a myriad eyes, but it is still I who see. Here, as in worship, in love, in moral action, and in knowing, I transcend myself; and am never more myself than when I do.

—C. S. Lewis

References

Every effort has been made to give sources for the quotations. In some cases, however the words have been around for so long that they have become beacons of culture that stand on their own. Some quotations have been gleaned over years of teaching and reading—they have long since become so much part of our mental furniture that we have lost track of the particular article or book where we first discovered them. We hope that these references will stimulate the reader to explore and delight in the wealth of material on children's literature and on books in general.

All verses from the Bible are in the New International Version unless otherwise noted.

Cover

The cover painting is *The Grandmother Tree* (oil on canvas, 40 x 30 inches) by Rose Mewhort (photographed by Helen Elizabeth Schnare). The model for this tree is a weather-worn Douglas fir high on the bluffs of Galiano Island, British Columbia.

Dedication

This wonderful and wise initial quotation is the first line of Neil Postman's introduction to his book THE DISAPPEARANCE OF CHILDHOOD, Vintage, 1994, p. xi.

*Re*story*ing*

The initial quotes are from Alasdair MacIntyre in AFTER VIR-
TUE: A STUDY IN MORAL THEORY, Notre Dame, 1984, p. 216
and Northrop Frye in THE EDUCATED IMAGINATION, Indiana,
1964, pp. 48 and 69. Frye's book is a good basic introduction to his view
of literature and to his ideas on the centrality of the Biblical narrative for
an understanding of literature. See also his thorough study of the Biblical
pattern for literature in THE GREAT CODE: THE BIBLE AND LIT-
ERATURE.

In the beginning of **Restorying** we use again the initial quote from
Alasdair MacIntyre. And from Northrop Frye's same book (pp. 110
and 111) comes yet another affirmation of the Bible as the beginning
point for understanding story in literature.

In J. R. R. Tolkien's epilogue to "On Fairy-Stories" in THE
TOLKIEN READER (Ballantine, 1966, pp. 71-73), he discusses the way
in which the "Eucatastrophe" or happy ending of the Bible story serves as
the consummate pattern for all the tales we tell:

> The Gospels contain a fairy-story, or a story of a larger kind which
> embraces all the essence of fairy stories. They contain many marvels—
> peculiarly artistic, beautiful, and moving: and among the marvels is the
> greatest and most complete conceivable eucatastrophe. But this story
> has entered History and the primary world: the desire and aspiration of
> sub-creation has been raised to the fulfillment of Creation. The Birth of
> Christ is the eucatastrophe of Man's history. The Resurrection is the
> eucatastrophe of the story of the Incarnation. This story begins and
> ends in joy. It has pre-eminently the "inner consistency of reality."
> There is no tale ever told that men would rather find was true . . . The
> Christian joy, the *Gloria*, is . . . pre-eminently high and joyous. But
> this story is supreme; and it is true. Art has been verified. God is the
> Lord, of angels, and of men—and of elves. Legend and History have
> met and fused . . . The Evangelium has not abrogated legends; it has
> hallowed them, especially the "happy ending."

G. K. Chesterton's essay "The Ethics of Elfland," in ORTHODOXY,
Doubleday, 1936, p. 61, is really an apologetic for a belief in God—the
magician of the magic in fairytales and the storyteller behind all the stories of our lives.

References

The quote from Gary Schmidt's book THE SIN EATER (Dutton, 1996, p. 159) is only one of his many profound insights into the place of story in our lives. Schmidt is Professor of English at Calvin College where he teaches Children's Literature.

In "On Fairy-Stories" Tolkien talks about the "Soup" of story:

> Speaking of the history of stories and especially of fairy-stories we may say that the Pot of Soup, the Cauldron of Story, has always been boiling, and to it have continually been added new bits, dainty and undainty." (pp. 26-27)

Jane Yolen uses the same image when talking about all that goes into a child's mind (see the tenth reason for "Family Reading").

The end of **Restorying** refers to Henry Zylstra, long-time teacher of English at Calvin College and writer of a superb book on the relationship of the Christian to secular culture. In discussing literature as a source for maturing a Christian's view of life, Zylstra affirms ("Why read Novels?" in TESTAMENT OF VISION, Eerdman's, 1961, p. 57):

> There is a real sense in which it [the novel] enables us by vicarious experience in our life to bring to bear on being Christian, myriads of lives not our own. I suppose the way the philosophers would say it is this, that by universalizing ourselves in the significant experience of others there is more of us that is Christian, that can be Christian, than there was before. There is more of you, after reading Hardy, to be Christian with than there was before you read him, and there is also more conviction that you want to be it.

Introducing Young Children to Books

The initial quotes are from Kornei Chukovsky (we've lost the source for this quote—Chukovsky is not only the Father of Russian Literature for Children, but has been tremendously influential in helping us be aware of the value of literature in the lives of our children) and Dorothy Butler in her excellent and very helpful book, BABIES NEED BOOKS, Bodley Head, 1980, pp. 10 and 11.

Picture Books

G. K. Chesterton penned this bit of quintessential Chesterton in a picture book he gave to a young child; we present it as the initial quote for the "Picture Books" section and as a solid defence of the picture book for children.

In the section "All About Animal Anthropomorphism," the quotation in the entry under Beatrix Potter is from a letter to a friend before the publication of THE TALE OF PETER RABBIT referring to her disagreements with the potential publisher over the size and cost of her books (in A HISTORY OF THE WRITINGS OF BEATRIX POTTER by Leslie Linder, Frederick Warne, 1971, p. 94).

Poetry

The initial quotes are from C. S. Lewis, AN EXPERIMENT IN CRITICISM, Cambridge, 1992, p. 103; Jim Trelease in THE READ-ALOUD HANDBOOK, Penquin, 1982, p. 61; and Calvin Ryan in "Reading to my Daughter," THE HORNBOOK, April 1952.

The quote in the introduction from Eugene Peterson is in ANSWERING GOD: THE PSALMS AS TOOLS FOR PRAYER, Harper and Row, 1989, p. 11.

Bible Stories

The initial quotes are from Northrop Frye, THE EDUCATED IMAGINATION, Indiana, 1964, p. 70; Dorothy Sayers, THE MAN BORN TO BE KING, Harper and Row, 1943, pp. 21 and 22; and Eugene Peterson's translation of the Gospels in THE MESSAGE.

Three very helpful sources for increasing understanding of the great literary gift we have in THE BIBLE are J. R. R. Tolkien's "On Fairy-Stories," in THE TOLKIEN READER and Northrop Frye's books, THE EDUCATED IMAGINATION and THE GREAT CODE: THE BIBLE AND LITERATURE.

References

Fairy Tales and Mythology

The initial quotes are from G. K. Chesterton, "The Ethics of Elfland," ORTHODOXY; Katherine Paterson, THE SPYING HEART, E. P. Dutton, 1989, p. 28 and J. R. R. Tolkien, "On Fairy-Stories," THE TOLKIEN READER, Ballantine, 1966, p. 3.

For more information on the background of Cinderella and a very helpful introduction to fairy tales, see Iona and Peter Opie's THE CLASSIC FAIRY TALES, Oxford, 1974. In their section on Cinderella, they mention the earliest version as one written in a Chinese book of 850-860 A.D. However, a picture book version of the story, THE EGYPTIAN CINDERELLA by Shirley Climo, is taken from the old tale of a Greek slave girl Rhodopis recorded in the first century B.C. by a Roman historian named Strabo. The slave girl was a real person who married the Pharoah Amasis around 570-526 B.C.

The wisdom of Marcia Brown is helpful for defending any book of fiction that has a keen sence of the struggle of darkness and light in human life, but is particularly apropos to fairy tales and fantasy where the extremes are cosmic in their intensity. The quotation at the end of this introduction is from her book, LOTUS SEEDS: CHILDREN, PICTURES AND BOOKS, Charles Scribner's, 1986, p. 54.

Fantasy and Science Fiction

The initial quotes are from Tolkien's essay "On Fairy-Stories," p. 54 (quoting from a verse letter to the still non-Christian C. S. Lewis); and George MacDonald's long-out-of-print book, A DISH OF ORTS. CHIEFLY PAPERS ON THE IMAGINATION, AND ON SHAKSPERE [*sic*], Sampson Low Marston, 1895, p. 28. Two wonderful essays in this book make it worth tracking down in a rarebooks room of a library: "The Imagination: Its Functions and Culture" (the source of this wonderful quote on the imagination and—by implication—on imaginative writing of the sort found in fantasy) and "The Fantastic Imagination."

A very helpful book on understanding the place and impact of fantasy in modern life is Ursula K. Le Guin's book THE LANGUAGE OF THE NIGHT: ESSAYS ON FANTASY AND SCIENCE FICTION, G. P. Putnam's, 1980. The first quote in our introduction is from an essay of hers, "Prophets and Mirrors: Science Fiction as a Way of Seeing" quoted in that book (p. 31). In another essay, "The Child and the Shadow," she sums up her view of fantasy (as a defense of Tolkien from charges of escapism): " . . . fantasy is the natural, the appropriate, language for the recounting of the spiritual journey and the struggle of good and evil in the soul" (p. 68).

The quoted phrases in the entry under Ursula K. Le Guin on TOMBS OF ATUAN are from Marcia Brown, LOTUS SEEDS: CHILDREN, PICTURES, AND BOOKS.

Animal Stories

The initial quote is from the poem "Impenitence" from C. S. Lewis, POEMS, edited by Walter Hooper, Harcourt Brace, 1964, p. 2.

Historical Fiction

The initial quotes are from Rosemary Sutcliff's essay "History is People," in CHILDREN AND LITERATURE: VIEWS AND REVIEWS, edited by Virginia Haviland, Scott Foresman, 1973, p. 311; Penelope Lively in "Children and Memory," THE HORNBOOK, August 1973, pp. 403 and 402; and T. S. Eliot in "Four Quartets, THE COMPLETE POEMS AND PLAYS: 1909-1950. The two articles by Sutcliff and Lively are excellent introductions to historical fiction for children.

The sea stories by Patrick O'Brian start with MASTER AND COMMANDER and go on for twenty volumes that build up a hearty respect for the exploits of the British Navy in the early 1800's; most young people would prefer the Horatio Hornblower series by C. S. Forester. Both sets of books deal with the realities of human joys and failings as well as with high adventure.

The Sutcliff quote is again from "History is People," p. 306.

Good Stories

Kit Pearson's description of finding a good book is from AWAKE AND DREAMING, Viking, 1996, p. 16.

References

Prolific Authors for Avid Readers

The initial quote is from C. S. Lewis, "On Juvenile Tastes," in OF OTHER WORLDS: ESSAYS AND STORIES, Harcourt Brace, 1966, p. 39.

In the introduction we quote from J. I. Packer's article, "Tecs, Thrillers, and Westerns," in CHRISTIANITY TODAY, November 8, 1985, p. 12.

Helps Along the Way to Good Books for Children

The initial quotes are from C. S. Lewis's "On Three Ways of Writing for Children," in OF OTHER WORLDS, edited by Walter Hooper, Harcourt Brace, 1966, pp. 24 and 28; Grahame Greene's THE LOST CHILDHOOD AND OTHER ESSAYS, Viking, 1962, p. 13; and Elizabeth Goudge's A CITY OF BELLS, Gerald Duckworth, 1936, p. 105.

Under "Family Reading" in the tenth reason for reading aloud we quote Jane Yolen from "Makers of Modern Myths," THE HORNBOOK, October 1975, p. 497.

Flannery O'Connor has some excellent advice for how to read contemporary literature in her book MYSTERY AND MANNERS: OCCASIONAL PROSE, selected and edited by Sally and Robert Fitzgerald, Farrar, Straus and Giroux, 1970. This book and her letters in THE HABIT OF BEING are not only fascinating reading, but offer a liberal arts education in the interpretation and meaning of imagery in literature. The two quotations from O'Connor in the section "Parental Guidance Suggested" are both from the essay "Catholic Novelists and Their Readers" in MYSTERY AND MANNERS, p. 188.

"The Potter Problem" is an attempt to go quickly to the heart of the matter—which is certainly the witchcraft content. That was the immediate turnoff that began the whole furor over these books. The issue is, however, a complex one and deserves a more thorough knowledge of the careful thinking that has characterized both sides of the issue. Here are some articles that help us understand the complexity of the issue.

Articles <u>not</u> in support of the Harry Potter books:

Kimbra Wilder Gish, "Hunting Down Harry Potter," THE HORN-BOOK, May/June 2000.

Alison Lentini, "Harry Potter: Occult Cosmology and the Corrupted Imagination" SCP [Spiritual Counterfeits Project] JOURNAL 23:4-24:1 (at *www.scp-inc.org*).

Articles in support of the Harry Potter books:

Alan Jacobs, "Harry Potter's Magic," FIRST THINGS, January 2000.

Gary D. Schmidt, "The Dangerous Harry Potter," CHRISTIAN HOME AND SCHOOL, March/April 2000.

The quotation that follows "Sources of Good Books" is from Katherine Paterson's book THE SPYING HEART: MORE THOUGHTS ON READING AND WRITING BOOKS FOR CHILDREN, E. P. Dutton, 1989, p. 37.

References

The initial quote is a statement on the meaning of reading from C. S. Lewis's very helpful book AN EXPERIMENT IN CRITICISM, Cambridge, 1965, pp. 140-141.

Index

Authors

177

Illustrators

A TIME TO READ

Titles

214

Printed in the United States
29357LVS00006B/66